The Art of LIVING in your GREEN ZONE

The Art of LIVING in your GREEN ZONE

Lifelong-happiness and Relationships

DR. K. SOHAIL MBBS FRCP(C)

White Knight Publications
2002, Toronto, Canada

Published in 2002 by White Knight Publications
a division of Bill Belfontaine Ltd.
Suite 103, One Benvenuto Place
Toronto Ontario Canada M4V 2L1
416-925-6458 e-mail: whitekn@istar.ca

Distributed in Canada by Hushion House Distributors Ltd.
36 Northline Road Toronto Ontario Canada M4B 3E2
Telephone (416) 285-6100, Fax (416) 285-1777
Ordering: 1-905-873-2750

National Library of Canada Cataloguing in Publication Data

Sohail, K. (Khalid), 1952-
The art of living in your green zone : lifelong-happiness and relationships

ISBN 0-9730949-0-7

1. Interpersonal relations. I. Title.

HM1106.S63 2002 158.2 C202-902048-4

Cover and text design: Karen Petherick, Peterborough, Ontario
Editing : Bill Belfontaine, Toronto, Ontario

Printed and bound in Canada

DEDICATED TO …

The individuals, couples and families,

who, throughout their therapy,

inspired me to develop the healing philosophy

of the Green, Yellow and Red Zones.

ACKNOWLEDGEMENTS

Special thanks to Anne Aguirre

a co-traveller on my professional and

philosophic journey,

to Karen Petherick for her outstanding cover

and text design

and to my editor and friend, Bill Belfontaine,

for his devotion to this book

and unending sage advice.

CONTENTS

INTRODUCTION

Everyone Has A Special Gift

When I was a young boy I was quite a dreamer, totally fascinated by the life stories of philosophers, artists, mystics and writers. I believed that they knew the truth, the ultimate reality, that they could heal suffering souls and provide insight into the dilemmas of human existence. I believed that those individuals changed the course of history and that they were ahead of their time. I thoroughly enjoyed their biographies and having passionate discussions about their lives and philosophies with all who would involve themselves in these discussions. In my imagination, I enjoyed living amongst them, reaching out to know more, reaching out to the unknown.

When I achieved my late teenage years, my mother encouraged me to become a doctor and I entered medical school with my thoughts concentrated on it as a healing profession. But soon I found myself in conflict. During daytime studies I was taught Anatomy, Pathology and Medicine and in the evenings my thoughts turned to the study of literature, religion and philosophy. I started writing short stories and poems as well, causing my mother to become upset. "Sohail! You have your Anatomy exam tomorrow and you are writing poetry. How is this going to help you pass?" I'd smile sheepishly and sometimes admit to my shortcomings; at other times I became quite angry at the attitude of this interfering, yet well-meaning and concerned woman. Fortunately, and with the help of a good recall system in my memory, I never failed an examination, so our conflict never reached a crisis point.

As a medical graduate some years later, I found myself at a crossroads with many dreams to be fulfilled. The first was to become a writer, the second to travel and experience the wide world, and finally, to specialize in a profession I loved. I could not envision myself practising medicine or surgery for the rest of my life. The specialization that would encompass all my interests proved to be psychiatry.

Since this part of the healing art shares borders with medicine, psychology, sociology and philosophy and is ever enquiring, I chose this fascinating field for my life's work. I found the ever-broadening subject forever exciting as it attempts to solve the mysteries of the human condition. Solve one mystery and another would always appear waiting to be addressed. I was quite surprised, and somewhat disappointed, that many medical graduates entered into psychiatry, not because they liked it, but because they could not achieve their goals in another specialization. Even after entering the psychiatric field I was less interested in the physical functioning of the brain and more interested in the essence of human beings, the mind, the personality and the character.

I was pleased to discover that the word "psyche" used to mean "soul" before it was transformed to "mind" by

Western psychologists. My interests in the abstract, the meaning of life and the evolution of human beings led me to become more deeply rooted in the specialty of being a psychotherapist. Becoming one also helped me to grow in the artistic and personal aspect of my life that remained as part of my dreams for the future.

Over the years I have reflected on many matters and have chosen a life based on Humanistic Philosophy. To me, Psychiatry and Humanism are two sides of the same coin, reflecting two aspects of my life and my personality. As a Humanist I am free to question the accepted, a freedom that allows my daily growth to continue unchecked, while respect remains for all that has come before.

The first step in using such a philosophy in my clinical practice was my becoming aware of the concept, "Everyone has a special gift." I was introduced to this, over twenty years ago, by a most kindly teacher, Dr. Sotus Kotsopoulos, during my first year of psychiatric training at Memorial University, Newfoundland. It has remained as one of my guiding principles in therapy ever since. That was the phase in my life when I was a student full of enthusiasm and motivation but lacking in the experience from which sound judgement is created. I was fascinated with the discipline of psychotherapy but knew little if anything about this healing art and its application.

When I started my hands-on training in the Child and Adolescent Psychiatry Unit in Janeway Hospital, Dr. Kotsopoulos became my supervisor. He was a gentle, patient teacher and I felt very connected with him. After initial introductions, he said we would assess a patient together, after which I was expected to see the patient alone and later on discuss every interview with him. I found it hard to contain my excitement. I felt as though I was going to learn to swim and he was my instructor with a life ring standing by, reassuring me that I could not drown. I trusted him so completely that I was very willing to jump into my ocean of self-doubt, and the opaque waters of the unknown.

The first patient was Julie, a teenage girl, who had a severe limp. Her family doctor, after thoroughly investigating her case, which included x-rays, blood and urine tests, etc., could not find a physical reason for her disability. He'd sent Julie to the psychiatric department for therapy as he believed it was "all in her head." When we first met she appeared to be quite shy but within a short time she felt comfortable being with us knowing we were there to help. She was a Grade 9 student who lived with her parents and Sarah, a year older sister, who in her opinion was "more beautiful, more intelligent and more popular" than she. At the end of the interview, when Dr. Kotsopoulos asked if she would like to see me regularly, she promptly agreed. He registered her and asked me to see her once a week for psychotherapy. A short time later we met in a small, comfortable office where I chose to wear casual clothing rather than a white coat so the traditional, clinical aspect of doctor/patient would be lessened.

I accepted the responsibility but felt utterly lost as I could not properly grasp how my talking to her would cure her limp. Her ailment was so obviously physical as one could see from a distance as she approached. For me, limping was a physical symptom and needed medical or surgical intervention. Dr. Kotsopoulos was very confident that psychotherapy would help her but I remained quite skeptical. I did not believe him in my heart of hearts but I lacked the confidence to disagree with him openly. I was trying very hard to maintain an open mind and allow him the benefit of the doubt, but it was most difficult to suppress the feeling.

Julie came every week for therapy sessions and talked about her parents, sister, friends and teachers. After watching her limp away following each session, I immediately met with Dr. Kotsopoulos to discuss my interview. Week after week I saw no progress in either Julie or myself, but Dr. Kotsopoulos was pleased that she was developing a trusting relationship with me which was leading her to increasingly and openly share her life story. As further weeks of therapy evolved, I was surprised to see this sweet young person showing anger, resentment and hostility towards her sister. She believed Sarah had ruined her life and eclipsed her happiness as she stood first in her class and was admired by everyone. She complained that Sarah was so beautiful, charming and outgoing that everybody in the school and neighbourhood wanted to be her friend, while Julie became more and more withdrawn. Julie was sick of being compared to her sister and fed up with being put down, ignored or barely tolerated by everyone. There were many times when she wondered whether she would have been happier if Sarah were not in her life.

I listened earnestly to Julie's complaints and expressions of her feelings, seeking the nuances of discovery that Dr. Kotsopoulos said I would find that would help her, and never for a moment losing my compassion for her ailment. But I had nothing to say that would help her. I was beginning to develop a feeling of inadequacy as a therapist as I had no advice to ease the suffering of this young woman. Yet I remained committed and anxious to help her in every way possible. My concern was also growing that Dr. Kotsopoulos would be disappointed in my performance because the results of the first few weeks of therapy produced no progress. No change came to her limping gait, although, thankfully, it did not deteriorate further.

Finally I asked Dr. Kotsopoulos to explain more fully what he saw my role to be in these therapy sessions, and what I was expected to accomplish. Dr. Kotsopoulos smiled and asked quite pointedly, "What does limping mean to Julie?" I remained without an answer after interviewing and studying her for weeks.

"What does this mean to you?" he asked again. Another simple but profound question. I remained silent, deep in concentration and offered no reply.

He shared his impressions, "I think Julie is suffering from sibling rivalry. She sees her sister getting all the attention in school and at home and the only way for her to get attention is by limping and adopting a sick role to elicit sympathy. Because of that ailment her parents took her to the doctor, had all kinds of tests done that provided no help, and finally she was brought to us. Because of her limping she got her parents' attention and is now getting more from you every week."

I was quite fascinated by such a formulation but I could not agree with it — nor was I prepared to argue his thesis as I could not really connect to it being the source of healing that Julie needed. I thought it was more of a reflection of Dr. Kotsopoulos's rich imagination than the patient's condition and I thought that even if I agreed with him, how would that help my patient's limping? How would that cure her suffering?

As weeks passed I felt more concerned and was filled

with a growing sympathy towards Julie. I passionately wanted her to get better and become less of a lonely and suffering soul. She considered herself ugly, clumsy and stupid while I saw her as a bright, intelligent and charming person and I told her so. Whenever I praised her and gave her a compliment she blushed and I could see her discomfort as she squirmed in her chair. She thought I was trying to be nice to her and saying all those wonderful things about her because it was my job to do so. But she could not understand what I saw in her attributes. I continued to remain lost in doubt. I blundered about in my frustration unable to find the right path to guide Julie to improved health.

Nearly three months passed and no letup of the limp had occurred. Like my patient, I too was feeling inadequate. When I shared my frustrations with Dr. Kotsopoulos, rather than being critical he was very supportive and asked me something that became a turning point in my therapeutic approach. "Every human being is unique. Nature has given all of us a special gift. What is the special gift life has given Julie?"

"I can't determine that."

"Help your patient to discover it. Then she can lead a happy and healthy life. She will have no need to limp to get attention. Discovering one's special gift is one of the significant goals of psychotherapy. It is like giving birth. The patient carries and delivers it with the therapist helping the patient to do so. In effect, you become the midwife."

Dr. Kotsopoulos's use of that particular analogy further showed his brilliance, knowing it would affect me more deeply. He knew that I had done my internship in obstetrics and delivered dozens of babies and that the joy of the feeling in my hands being the first to hold new life had never left me. That discussion was an eye-opener for me, the opening of an inner eye that has benefitted me so much as a healer. After that meeting, my attitude and approach towards Julie underwent a decided change.

I was no longer preoccupied with her sickness and symptoms. I began to focus on her healthy self and to discover her talents. I began to see her not as a patient but as an unfinished painting, a work of art in progress. It did not take me long to discover that she had a special talent in music and played piano far better than her sister. I encouraged her to play regularly, take special lessons and practise. She was quite thrilled with this new approach, one to which she could easily respond. The more she practised the better she became and the happier she felt. Her feeling better was expressed to me with an underlying enthusiasm that made me feel more inspired as a therapist. Dr. Kotsopoulos was pleased with my progress. He assured me that Julie had borrowed the courage to succeed and to grow beyond her ailment from our therapeutic relationship.

A few months later, Julie was invited to perform in front of hundreds of people during an annual celebration at the school. At the end of her excellent performance, the entire school audience, including her parents and sister, applauded enthusiastically. She was so ecstatic she jumped from the stage and ran to her family. Everyone was surprised to see that all evidence of limping had left her. From that evening onward she never limped again. Everybody felt proud of her and she felt so proud of herself, too. She was the successful local artist who had discovered the love of her life, the world of her piano.

Not only had she grown, I had grown with her too. Julie's discovery of her special gift of music allowed me to claim the true beginning of my special gift of being a psychotherapist. Dr. Kotsopoulos had helped us deliver our special talents in those few short months. He had become our midwife. How thankful we both were. Our therapy discussions soon came to an end. With Julie's success I felt proud to be a part of the healing profession.

Over the years I have continued to develop my special gift and pursue my fascination within the art and science of psychotherapy and the world surrounded by it. During the last decade I have become involved in writing and publishing professional, philosophical and literary works and also attending many conferences, workshops and seminars to share the Humanistic Philosophy of psychotherapy. I was quite thrilled to present a paper, "Psychotherapy with People Suffering from Schizophrenia," at the Canadian Psychiatric Association Annual meeting in Saskatchewan, Canada and a workshop, "Psychotherapy with Couples," at the International Conference on Divorce and Remarriage in Jerusalem, Israel. At a later workshop, "Psychotherapy with Immigrants," at the World Psychiatric Congress in Rio, Brazil, I was able to discuss my ideas, experiences and conceptual framework with colleagues from far-flung countries around the world.

I am inspired to share my ideas and experiences in a variety of books. The most recent focuses on my proven concept of the Green, Yellow, Red Zones based on my clinical work for more than two decades, with hundreds of individuals, couples, families and larger gatherings. The creation of these psychological zones helps me to better understand and to more completely explain the emotional states of people and the dynamics of their interpersonal relationships. This conceptual framework has also been very useful in helping people resolve or dissolve their conflicts. During this process they not only become more aware of their true selves and how to deal with their emotional problems more effectively, but also how to move toward improving the quality of their lives. Barriers are removed that prevented them from taking the first step toward leading happier and healthier lifestyles. They discover peace within themselves and harmony in their family, social, love and work relationship.

The winning ways of embracing the colour concept are simple but deeply profound. It is easy to grasp, but as one becomes aware of its different dimensions and complexities, one can modify and improvise, depending on one's personality, lifestyle, dilemmas and dreams and how one chooses to adapt to it so that it becomes part of their personality.

After using this successful concept in my professional life, I started sharing it with my colleagues and friends. I was pleasantly surprised that people who did not suffer from any emotional problems found it equally fascinating. It improved the quality of their relationships with their dear ones and with others in their social and professional communities. They helped to make me aware of the universality of the concept of living lives in the zones of different colours. It continues to be very rewarding to see increasing numbers of professionals and lay people improving the quality of their personal, family, social and work endeavours with this simple but profound concept.

This book is the first of the series in which I will be focusing on my Humanistic Philosophy and its application in clinical practice. In the future I will write to assist people suffering from specific conditions and facing specific dilemmas such as Depression, Schizophrenia, marital problems and immigrant integration difficulties. There are many debilitating, life-eroding illnesses, so prevalent in our fast-paced, disjointed society that can be dealt with and improved using this positive form of involvement.

By writing this book I choose to share the insights I have found, hoping to inspire others to begin to search for their own special gift. Such gifts bring a special meaning to our lives and provide us with an opportunity to serve humanity in general and our loved ones in particular.

By sharing our special gifts with others, we create a more wondrous human environment that the world so sorely needs, where all can live a fulfilling life in peace and harmony.

Part One

GREEN YELLOW RED ZONES

STEP BY STEP

Life's Journey is Best Taken One Step at a Time

To learn the art of living in your Green Zone, you have to understand the basic concept and then put it into practice by remaining aware of its benefits. Simply stated, I have made it easy for you to bridge the gap between theory and practice in ten practical steps that are easy to follow. They are simple, yet interesting guidelines to assist you to appreciate the process and to allow you to discuss the concepts with your family and close friends. These steps are easily-reached milestones on that significant journey which will improve your quality of life and make it much more meaningful once you have become tuned into the new life waiting ahead for you.

STEP ONE - Recognizing Your Emotional Zones

The first step on any journey towards the significant change being sought is that of awareness. When you become solidly aware of your emotional state, it is easier to improve it. Accordingly, you live in one of the states of your

Green, Yellow or Red Zones at any particular moment of your daily life. This applies to every human being.

When you live in the Green Zone you are pleasant and cheerful, looking forward to the day and its events being positive. You are capable of a free exchange of caring and affection with family, friends and co-workers. You are ready for a rational discourse with people around you and if there is a difference of opinion, you are able to have a healthy and constructive dialogue to resolve or dissolve conflicts, which will smooth out the bumpy road filled with differences. You remain communicative and don't feel slighted because what is being said is a positive influence on your attitude and relationships.

But when you are in the Yellow Zone you feel distressed. You can become anxious, sad and often angry. Because of this discomfort you are not able to communicate properly with others and are poorly equipped to deal with stressful situations or conflicts where an interpersonal solution is required.

Should you find yourself in the Red Zone, you have become extremely unhappy, often emotionally exhausted, very angry and almost always, depressed. You will sometimes lose control and become abusive and often completely withdrawn from others. They, as well as you, have great difficulty in dealing with the stressful situations that you or someone else in their Red Zone has caused. You find yourself unable to have a rational dialogue that could lead to resolving or dissolving your interpersonal conflicts. At times, in an extreme case, you may have reached the point where you are unwilling or unmotivated to take care of yourself to socially acceptable standards.

As you begin to use the colour zones to study and

work on your problems, you become aware of how much time in your day-to-day life you spend in each zone. You may come to the sad realization that a lot of time is wastefully spent in emotional turmoil with the ups and downs that come from varying between the Yellow and Red Zones.

During initial interviews in my clinic, when people begin to share their pressing problems, often openly expressing anxiety, depression or anger, I encourage them to become more positive by using the question, "When was the last time you felt you were leading a happy and healthy life?" Many people who have experienced or are in the midst of a crisis, tell me that they have been unhappy for weeks or even longer. Then there are others who say, and it still continues to shock me, "I have been unhappy all my life. I don't remember the last time I felt any joy." How sad that such potentially productive people have been living in a Yellow or Red Zone most of their lives. What a tragedy to have lived as a child, teen and adult, never knowing the happiness of living in the Green Zone, knowing only the vicious cycles: of the unhappiness so prevalent in the Yellow Zone and feeling especially morose in the failures of their Red Zone!

STEP TWO - Recognizing Your Communication Style

Since human beings are forever communicating with others, it is quite understandable that your emotional state is affected by your communication patterns. Becoming aware of your communication style helps you to begin to realize how your own emotional states are affected by the emotional states of your significant others at home, socially, or at work.

Through working with couples and helping them with

their marital conflicts, I have become convinced that for a healthy and constructive dialogue between two people, both parties need to be in their Green Zones. Distressing as it may sound, people remaining in their Red Zone are not very different than those who are intoxicated. You can argue but you cannot reason with them satisfactorily if you are seeking to obtain any long-term resolution. Waiting until both parties return to their Green Zones is the only satisfactory way for a healthy dialogue to resume.

It is not uncommon to observe in the beginning of a dialogue, that one person will be feeling quite secure in their Green Zone and trying to deal positively with someone who is deeply in their Red Zone. Yet, as the dialogue progresses with an opportunity to enter into a place of cooperation in the Green Zone, the one living in the Green Zone gradually feels less secure, is pulled lower and lower into their Yellow Zone and often ends in despair, frustration and anger in an embattled Red Zone. During that process both parties feel frustrated, angry or hurt, or all three sensations at the same time, and when both people are thrashing around in the Red Zone all progressive communication breaks down. Sometimes it takes hours, days and even weeks, each on their own time, to return to the Green Zone, the only place where it is possible to resume a healthy relationship using a constructive dialogue.

I always ask people to compile a list of their significant relationships and then review them openly and honestly, completely free of bias. It is important to know which relationships are in the Green Zone, which are failing in the Yellow and which are seriously suffering in their Red Zone. Once those relationships that are in the Yellow and Red Zones are identified, we become "partners" in our discussion of strategies for dealing with those non-productive relationships.

STEP THREE - Recognizing Changes in Your Emotional Zones

As you become aware of the colours of the emotional states, you start to take note of the changes in your day-to-day life. It is important to know and understand the significant factors, circumstances, or people that uproot you from a temperate Green Zone and push you into the Yellow and Red Zones that are similar to what they are occupying. There lies the first step in you taking responsibility for your healthy and happy Green Zone. By becoming aware of these colour Zones, you realize that you can have a serious dialogue or make important decisions only when both parties are also firmly established in their Green Zone.

STEP FOUR - Recovering from Yellow and Red Zones

After recognizing and understanding what zone you are living in, you also become aware how you can recover from your Yellow and Red Zones. You may wish to take time out from a negative situation by engaging in some form of physical activity, listening to soothing music, reading, visiting a friend, using your computer or playing with children to return to the positive, productive reality of your Green Zone. It takes a few minutes' concentration to find the way to come back, but it is well worth the effort.

In discovering what works for different people, I find it gives them more control to spend the least amount of time within the discomfort and failure of their Yellow Zone, or the Red Zone where distressing events often take place.

The most productive time happens when one's emotional state is firmly anchored in the Green Zone.

STEP FIVE - Restraining Yourself from Entering Yellow and Red Zones

After becoming aware of your style of Recognizing and Recovering, you will also learn ways of Restraining yourself from falling or being pushed into Yellow and Red Zones by people, stressful situations or circumstances that are often beyond your control. It is understandable for you to want to avoid those situations and the people who have such a negative effect on your otherwise happy outlook. If you cannot avoid them, go well prepared emotionally so that you become least affected. Plan your visit in such a way that if the interaction becomes too stressful you can leave. Such planning gives you more control in dealing with difficult situations that often end unhappily or become the source of additional stress.

STEP SIX - Recognizing Family Zones

As people become more aware of their emotional states, I consult with them to see how their family system affects their emotional state. When people realize that their particular family lives most consistently in the Yellow or Red Zone, they are ready to learn ways to cope with that by initiating a constructive dialogue to begin to help resolve or dissolve the conflicts. When they cannot resolve the conflict, I discuss how they can either accept their situation gracefully or leave the family system entirely. Many people function well in the Green Zone outside the home but when they encounter the family, it does not take much time for them to be drawn into the Yellow and Red Zones. The family as a whole lives there and refuses, or doesn't know how, to leave the "comfort of their discomfort." People gradually realize that like individuals, families also live in different Zones. So theoretically we can have Green, Yellow and Red families. Red Zone families provide the atmosphere of a toxic environment that affects everybody who enters their emotional system. People gradually realize that these systems are emotionally far stronger and more powerful than individuals.

STEP SEVEN - Recognizing Work Zones

In addition to a family system, most people are also exposed to an employment system on a regular basis. Before you can deal with work problems in a constructive way, it is important to understand whether your work environment is established in a Green, Yellow or Red Zone. After study, when you become aware that you work in the Yellow and Red Zone, you have to think seriously about how to dispense with the conflicts, and if you cannot, whether you have the ability to live within the situation gracefully. Should that not be possible, it would be wise to consider leaving that toxic work environment to seek more fulfilling employment, for your long-term health.

STEP EIGHT - Recognizing Social Community Zones

Alongside the family and work systems people also interact with others in many social systems. Such systems include the neighbourhood and community. People who are active in any social, religious or political organization must become aware in what Zone each organization operates. Such awareness can help to create a personal plan to deal with that type of environment. Sharing the concept of

Green, Yellow, Red Zones with others in your groups might be a way to open up the channels of communication that can help in dissolving or lessening the conflicts. If that is not possible, then you have to consider either accepting the situation gracefully or planning to resign from the organization. Considering different options in itself gives you a realistic sense of power and control in your life. Look seriously at your need for seeking pleasure amongst people where there really is a problem for you.

STEP NINE - Requesting Help from a Mediator or Therapist

When you try to handle conflicts on your own, but are not successful, it would be wise to consider a mediator for social and political situations, or a therapist in marital and family dilemmas, before giving up your role in the relationship. If the mediator or the therapist can help to achieve a Green Zone relationship between you and the other party in a structured session, it then becomes possible to have a discussion that may correct the conflicts. Such intervention may bring the original relationship back to the Green Zone. The least it will do is improve the relationship.

STEP TEN - Learning to Enter, Stay and Live in the Green Zone

As you follow these initial steps on your journey to a better life, it becomes natural for you first to seek to enter the Green Zone for short periods of time. As time passes, you will find it easier to have more hours living in this happier state of mind. Your greater happiness will affect those around you, too. Many people we worked with found, within a few months, that they were living quite consistently in the Green Zone. How unfortunate that many had never before found the quality of life that would permit their lives to be spent in the Green Zone. Living there starts at the emotional level and soon extends to the family, social and work environments. It is not uncommon for people to discuss this concept with those who are close to them and to try to correct their conflicts. When they find that resolution cannot be achieved, they have the strength and patience either to accept the situation or to leave it temporarily or permanently.

Once you are motivated to seek the newness of change and are willing to follow these ten steps, within a few weeks you'll find yourself spending more time in the Green Zone emotionally and within a few months, you can look back on a most satisfying lifestyle change. You will have to learn to accept gracefully those situations that you cannot change. In time, a peaceful life will flow throughout your Self that creates a more harmonious life in your family, social and work environments. Such a change provides a new purpose and your life becomes more meaningful. It comes back to you as other people reflect back to you the brighter benefit you are giving them.

How exciting it has been for me to see the miraculous difference people have made of their lives by using this concept and understanding their emotional colours. How rewarding to see a new healthy and happy lifestyle being unveiled and to be there to watch people growing as individuals and families.

Such an approach to better mental health, and to life itself, has developed from the Humanistic Philosophy that I use in my practice as well as in my creative and adventurous personal life. According to this philosophy, as human beings we must carry the responsibility for improving our lifestyles and making our tomorrows better than our yesterdays whether individually or collectively. I am always comforted that not only have I discovered *The Art of Living in Your Green Zone* in my personal, social and work relationships, but that others are finding it a most meaningful long-term experience as well.

RECOGNIZING YOUR EMOTIONAL ZONES

The first step in *The Art of Living in Your Green Zone* is to develop the awareness of your emotional Zones. I strongly recommend that a daily diary be kept to record the changes in your emotional states, and if possible, the factors causing such states to occur. Within a few days of recording frank entries, you will be able to identify the Zone in which you are spending the most time.

It is somewhat disappointing for me to discover that not only do many people spend most of their time in the Yellow or Red Zone but also that they are not aware of its terrible grip on their attitudes and daily lives.

Their dear ones had tried in their own way to bring it to their attention but they never took the time to understand those concerns. But by keeping an unbiased record they came to the sad and profound realization of how they had been spending their emotional lives. When I meet people who were living in the Yellow and Red Zones for a long time, I found that many had grown up in Yellow and Red Zone families. During interviews, often of some length, I realized the following characteristics were inherent in their personalities and lifestyles.

Personal Life • They suffered from low, or very low, self-esteem and self-confidence and had been leading a chronically unhappy life. It was not uncommon for them to think that life was not worth living and many of them contemplated the ultimate tragedy — suicide.

Family Life • They did not have the opportunity to enjoy loving relationships with family members. In the past, many experienced abuse or neglect. Their role models were unhealthy in habits, deeds and attitude. It was very difficult for them to initiate and maintain intimate relationships as adults because they never experienced it throughout their formative years.

Social Life • They had difficulty making and maintaining friendships as they were unable to engage in healthy communication. For them, resolving and dissolving interpersonal conflicts was never easy. Often the only way they knew how to live was being the initiator or recipient of a power play of one personality over another.

Professional Life • They had difficulty finishing school which created a habit of failure and insecurity making it difficult for them to keep a job for any length of time. Many never achieved their full potential academically and professionally, or in anything else they tried to accomplish.

Recreational Life • They had difficulty relaxing and enjoying the casual and sports side of life. The local bar or tavern often became their height of socializing.

No opportunity was made to discover the fun part of life. They were in a constant struggle, feeling life was full of suffering, conflict and pain. They experienced their lives more as a constant conflict — a curse rather than a blessing.

Creative Life • Many became so conditioned by their upbringing that they were never able to learn how to get in touch with their creative self. They could not follow their intellectual passions and dreams or open their minds to the greater world that comes with being creative.

Purpose and Meaning in Life • They had no sense of direction or ability to establish worthwhile goals. They encountered difficulty in finding meaning and purpose in the hours of their day. They often lacked commitment to themselves, their families, friends and communities. Their lives seemed meaningless and life was perceived as worthless, and they often had no idea of the shallowness of their values.

Physical and Mental Health • Many suffered from serious physical or emotional problems and had a difficult time coping day by day or even hour by hour. Many lived like that all their lives, while others were fortunate to find friends, lovers or therapists who encouraged them to feel hope and understand the support given. This support can help them to discover their Green Zone where there is the opportunity to lead happy productive lives.

One such person was Sharon, a 31-year-old mother of a little girl. Her striking blonde looks and jocular manner concealed deep reservoirs of depression and mistrust. When I met Sharon, I felt concerned about her lifelong struggle but on the other hand I was quite impressed that, in spite of living in a chaotic family environment, there was a part of her personality that remained untouched by its negativity. She had maintained an island of Green Zone in the ocean of the debilitating Red Zone in which her family and friends functioned. Her Green Zone provided an oasis of peace and focus that let her finish high school, and provided the courage needed to leave home for a different province and finally encouraged her to seek professional help. When I asked her to share her story, it was a chronicle of suffering and despair that she was able to end in hope and happiness.

Dr. Sohail

Most of my life I have lived in the Red Zone. My childhood was horrible. There were nine siblings, three disabled in various ways. Father was gone, mostly working. When he was home he never paid much attention to his children. I always remember him as a very hardworking man. I loved my father but I was never close to him.

My mother was constantly cooking, cleaning, scrubbing, washing, baking, and all the while screaming at all of us that we made her sick and she wished that we were never born. She always told us we were ugly and good for nothing. She had her favourite, her eldest son Don. She always praised him. She seemed to treat certain ones differently. I always suspected that but never said anything. I did not really realize how true it was until my sister Jackie mentioned it once not very long ago that our mother singled me out and treated me very badly. I almost died when I was born. I needed blood transfusions to survive. I recall her all through my childhood telling me that I had the Devil's Blood. Jackie baby-sat us a lot. She told me I was a very quiet child. I always looked sad and scared. I was always afraid of my mother. She was forever hitting, a smack here and there and sometimes a good pinch, but that was just the way it was. She did not do it so much around my father because he got upset with her.

When I was ten, I went to live with my brother and his wife and their two-year-old daughter. This was my oldest brother Don. I loved him and I was his favourite. Everyone called me "Don's girl." But his wife treated me terribly when he was not around. She told me my housework and cooking was never good enough. I had to cook, clean and baby-sit until she got home. They split up when I was fifteen. She moved about half-an-hour away and I went with her. I was a virtual prisoner. I was not allowed to see any of my family anymore. I was not even allowed to attend my grandmother's funeral. My family did not do anything about it. My mother wanted me gone. My father did not talk to me for one year even when I tried to contact him because I did not attend his mother's funeral. He thought I did not care, not knowing that I was not allowed. I loved my grandmother but my sister-in-law would not let me go. I was afraid of her, too, and never stood up to her.

Finally my brother and her got divorced and one

weekend when she was away with her daughter and new boyfriend, I phoned my dad to come and get me and he did. I never went back.

When my dad brought me home, my mom lost it. She cried and said she did not want me there. I had just finished grade eleven. I had one more year of my high school left so for that year I sometimes slept at my parents' house (I used to sneak in late at night and sleep on the couch) or I stayed at my brother Don's or sister Jackie's house from time to time. I even stayed with my friends or even in my dad's truck. There was not a place for me. I do not know how I finished my school. My mother was always angry with me. One day she threw a fork at me and cut my eye. My parents had a big fight over that. After I finished Grade 12, I spent the summer just hanging around here and there. I had an older boyfriend who was very nice to me, but I was trying to figure out how I was going to get out of this town and this life that I hated so much. That was when I decided to sell my flute.

My last night in town, I stayed at my parents' place. My dad came in around 6:30 a.m. before leaving for work. He gave me a kiss and pressed $150 into my hand, that is why I still have my flute. I left around one in the afternoon. I remember looking out the window to see my two younger sisters and younger brother go back to school after lunch. A stranger gave me a ride to the airport. No one said goodbye to me.

I got to Toronto airport around 2:00 a.m. because everything got screwed up with the flights and the weather so I had to bus it from Ottawa. After getting to the airport I called the guy who I was supposed to be staying with. I had grown up next door to him. Weeks earlier he had said it was fine but his girlfriend answered the phone and said, "NO WAY!" So I was stuck at the airport at 2:00 a.m. A stranger who I had noticed looking at me in Halifax airport and had sat next to me on the way from Ottawa saw me sitting there by myself. I told him my situation and he offered me a stay at his place. I accepted his offer as I was not going to go back to Newfoundland.

I stayed there for a week and then went to live with a cousin I had never met before. He was an awful person; he just wanted my money. I was there for nearly two months and then I took a job selling encyclopedias. So I spent the next year and a half on the road. The rest was just one big mistake. I felt loneliness, anger, and confusion. I was one lost soul wandering around, trying to find some direction and never having any luck. Till this day I still have no direction.

I feel worthless but I know I should not. I want to be happy. I want to make my future better, that is why I came to see you, to get some help, some sense of direction. I need to get rid of my past ... badly!"

Working with Sharon confirmed my belief that everyone has a part deep inside that is like a seed. When a seed gets proper care (sunshine, fresh air and clean water) it grows like a lotus and rises above the marshes, a beautiful flower; without nourishment, it fails.

It can be a long journey from the Red Zone to the Green Zone but in the end it is worth every step that you take. I will discuss that journey in greater detail in future chapters.

RECOGNIZING YOUR COMMUNICATION STYLE

Once they understand their Emotional Zones, I encourage people to become aware of their communication style and what happens when they interact with people who use a different method of communication. I have been observing such interaction in marital therapy sessions especially.

It has been fascinating to see how women communicate so differently than men. With many couples, I see men talking in a logical and rational manner while women communicate from an emotional direction. Such a fundamental difference in style can be a source of frustration for either side and can push the communication efforts of the couple into the Yellow Zone. It can then easily sink to the disharmony so common in the Red Zone if they are not patient and do not remain observant as to what is occurring emotionally. To bring that to the attention of one couple, I wrote the following letter.

Dear Dawn and Solomon

After being married for twenty-five years, both of you wonder why you still have problems communicating with each other. Why is it that whenever you try to talk to each other, the dialogue turns into a heated discussion, discussion into debate and a debate into an argument and within no time you get angry, raise your voices and start verbally fighting? At the end of your arguments you are both emotionally bruised and the issue you started to discuss never gets resolved.

You have asked my impression about your different styles of communication and what can be done to improve them. I have listened to you talk with each other and I have talked to you separately. It seems to me that when you talk to me you are different people than when you talk to each other. Why is that? You are no different from many other couples who come to talk to us. It seems at times as if you belong to separate worlds. Both of you speak the same words but their meaning becomes different when you are listening to them. If someone asked me how both of you communicate I would say, "Like many men, Solomon speaks the language of the head while Dawn uses emotion and intuition and speaks the language of her heart. Solomon presents the objective point of view while Dawn comes forward with the subjective."

If both of you had the same style there would be no problem. It is interesting that neither of you has communication problems with your friends. It is fascinating to see how each of you perceives the other's style.

Dawn says, "He is not available emotionally."

Solomon says, "She is so sentimental, so hysterical, I tune her out."

With such perceptions I am not surprised that both of you feel misunderstood by the other.

When I listen to you, I feel as if Dawn is a novelist who likes to share all the details while Solomon is a short story writer who is very economical and does not want to waste words. Sometimes he even expresses himself telegraphically. That is why he becomes impatient listening to Dawn's detailed descriptions. He wants to know the bottom line and when Dawn does not get to it quickly, he tunes her out and that makes Dawn very frustrated. A couple of times he fell asleep while she was talking. She became so angry she felt like hitting him but instead, and wisely, she went for a long walk to cool down her anger.

I am sharing these impressions so that we can focus on your communication styles when I meet with you next week.

Sincerely,
Sohail

Couples who have problems with communicating have to learn the differences between the Green style and Red style of communication. With those using the Green Zone style of communication there is spontaneous sharing and feedback and the interaction can go on and on comfortably and enjoyably when patience and understanding is used. People who have Green Zone relationships easily resolve conflicts.

In the Yellow Zone style of communication conflicts emerge; the exchange of sharing and feedback is blocked and tension is created. Differences turn into verbal sparring and if the relationship sinks into their Red Zones, neither party can find the patience and civility to sort out the differences. Often the cooling-off period is quite lengthy.

Becoming aware of your communication style and the nature of your significant relationships is the proper path for you to follow. It will change your life and the way you interact with those you choose to share in your life and dreams.

Part Two

GREEN YELLOW RED ZONE

RELATIONSHIPS

GREEN YELLOW RED ZONE RELATIONSHIPS

Like individuals, relationships also have a personality, character and lifestyle. They are born, they grow, and they die, by separation, divorce or death. Intimate relationships have a life cycle of their own. I encourage people to assess the quality of their relationships and discover the Zone they are living in.

Healthy relationships thrive in the Green Zone and have Green Zone communication styles. In such relationships people feel free to spontaneously express their affection and are able to resolve their conflicts.

Unhealthy relationships live in the Yellow and Red Zones. In such relationships people feel inhibited and tense. Seldom is there a free flow of feelings and the differences turn into conflicts. In such relationships, resolving the problems becomes very difficult and in many cases people need a mediator or a therapist to assist them to find their way.

Many couples do not realize that they might well be able to solve their problems if they were to get proper professional help. In many cases, one of the spouses, realizing that the relationship is in trouble, suggests therapy but the other is reluctant, and often angrily so, which leads to the benefits of the therapy not being discussed. The relationship limps along in the Yellow or Red Zone until it encounters a crisis that either pushes them apart for good or propels them to the office of a therapist.

RESOLVING/DISSOLVING INTERPERSONAL CONFLICTS

While working with couples who choose to improve the quality of their interpersonal communication and seek to have a happier and healthier relationship, I share with them some of the mechanisms by which the spouse in the Red Zone pulls the other, who is often in the Green Zone, down into the Red Zone. By being aware of those mechanisms, they can recover from their present problems and restrain themselves from functioning in the Red Zone.

One such mechanism is called "taking the bait." The persons in the Red Zone can become so frustrated or angry that they throw out a comment that becomes the bait that the other cannot resist. In no time both are battling in the Red Zone either with loud, biting sarcasm or in complete silence.

I share with them three of the most common ways spouses throw out a bait that they know will provoke a reaction in the other person.

Accusations

Rather than sharing one's feelings by saying, "I feel sad," or "I feel hurt," or "I feel disappointed," the person in the Red Zone remarks, often not too gently, "You were so cruel yesterday," or "You offended me last night," or "You insulted me when we visited your parents." When people properly share feelings from the Green Zone, it gives the other person the opportunity to offer support. But when accusations start to fill the air, others become defensive and in many cases start their slide on the slippery slope at the edge of the Green Zone that ends in the Red Zone. Accusations can become irresistible bait, often containing a barbed hook that's hard to remove, and that most people have trouble resisting.

Generalizations

I've met many spouses who, rather than saying to their significant other, "Last night when I was talking to you, you seemed lost in your own world," prefer to jump in with both feet and say accusingly, "You never listen to me," or "You always ignore me," or "You think all women are stupid!" Such statements never help to solve problems; in fact they do just the opposite. Rather than focusing on a specific incident or behaviour for the purpose of problem solving, they launch a broad attack on the person's character and attitudes.

Bringing up the past

One sure way of pushing your communications into the Red Zone is to attempt to get the upper hand by raising past sins or omissions. If the grieved one feels they are not getting the type of attention they seek, they may be tempted to remind the other person of their failings in previous instances when the problem was being discussed. The issue that needs addressing gets lost in a general, often worthless, rehashing of the problems from before.

Exploiting Vulnerabilities

Most people have unresolved issues. Inevitably we become

aware of these sensitive areas in the personalities of the people we are close to, and those sensitivities can potentially serve as weapons if we choose to use them. I call these areas "sore elbows" or "bruised knees." We can be respectful and not touch those areas or we can push or jab at them, which will elicit a predictable angry response just like it did previously. Couples living in the Green Zone respect each other's sore knees while other couples, in their anger while being in the Red Zone, are compelled to jab at these sore spots through subtle hints or outright sarcasm. Those who are wounded will quickly realize what is happening and complain, "You certainly know how to push my buttons!"

The following page of a letter from a husband to his wife helps us to understand how damaging pushed buttons can be.

Dearest

After our fight on Sunday, I thought a lot about how we started out fine and then the conversation really deteriorated. That seems to be a pattern with us. Thinking it over, I realized that whenever we try to discuss disciplining Sherri, I seem to hurt you by bringing up your past drug problems. You worked hard to overcome them, and I guess I get so worried about Sherri that I want you to be more strict with her. You want to let her do many things that I wouldn't support, so I can't help reminding you of how you used to live and what happened to you. Then you get mad about that and we end up fighting about the past instead of dealing with Sherri. I feel really bad about that. I promise that in the future I will keep the discussion focused on what we're trying to do about Sherri and respect your feelings about a closed chapter of your life.

Love, Robert

RESOLVING YOUR INTIMATE RELATIONSHIP

There are many couples who had a happy and healthy marriage in the beginning and lived happily in the Green Zone, but over the years because of stresses and crises affecting their lives, and growing differences in their personalities and maturity, became frustrated, angry and often withdrawn. Because they could not resolve their conflicts their relationship fell into the Yellow Zone and finally dropped into the many unpleasant scenarios that abound in the Red Zone. Many such couples either lived chronically unhappy lives or decided to separate and divorce. I met a number of these couples and tried to help them save their marriage and family unit. Therapy helped them to return to their Green Zone. One such couple was Leslie and Barry. Leslie agreed to share the story of their relationship with me.

Dr. Sohail

We were deep in the Red Zone. Marital therapy helped my husband and me clear up long-standing difficulties created by our different anger-management styles. With direct teaching of some simple concepts: Green/Yellow/ Red Zones and "Time Out," our relationship improved as we learned to communicate more effectively. I will attempt to show how we got into difficulty and how we both learned to sort out and resolve important differences using the aforementioned strategies. Let me start with how I fell apart and then attempt to show how the insight into our personal management styles plus skill learning and guided practice have literally given us a more serene, manageable life together.

My husband Barry gets angry quickly and forcefully. Stopping his anger is like trying to hold back a hurricane. For years I chose to avoid his anger, like hiding in the basement until the storm blows over. My extreme fear of his anger made me want to avoid talking about anything that might provoke him. This gave him carte blanche to spend all he wanted on luxury cars, golf and electronics while I compensated for his spending with measures of my own. My solution to the problem was based on the mistaken belief that if I managed the budget better and spent less on myself, our problems would somehow be over. I shopped at second hand stores, taught night school and summer school as well as holding a fulltime teaching job. Later I bought and sold a rental house and used the profit to pay off his credit card debt. I scrimped and saved to make ends meet. But of course the debts were not over (and could never be) because I wasn't solving the problem.

My problems compounded at school as well as at home. Kids got more difficult as the permissive pendulum swung to the extreme and I was forced to teach outside of my original subject areas. My official teaching subjects were Science and Physical Education and I was asked to teach English, History, Family Studies and Special Education. The curriculum changed and Grade 9 students were forced into single level classes to give them a chance to adjust to high school without being labelled by their public school as either capable or not capable of advanced curriculum studies. I just worked harder thinking that if I could simply teach perfect lessons, student behaviour would also improve. I was always anxious and stressed out and lived mostly in the Yellow Zone.

As our problems increased my resentment mounted and pleasure in life diminished to the point where I had to take time off school. I cried all the time and a perceptive friend remarked that I looked like a combat-weary soldier. Finally after being on leave from school with severe depression for four months and, living in the Red Zone, I left Barry and went to live with my mother. I felt free from work and marriage for the first time in twenty-eight years.

When I discussed my problems, you encouraged me to write a letter to Barry, sharing my perception of the problems. You offered marital, individual and group therapy to both of us. The shock of all this made Barry look at his life seriously and admit that his anger was interfering with other relationships as well as our own. I had decided to leave the marriage and had no intentions of going back, but when Barry agreed to get involved in therapy, I decided to give him the benefit of the doubt. So we attended regularly and began to renegotiate the terms of our twenty-eight-year marriage. We lived apart, dated each other and gradually learned the skills to manage anger and resolve conflicts.

One of the first skills we used was to shut up when a Time Out *was called by either of us. This was most effective when a simple referee's time-out hand signal was used [the upright fingers of one hand form a "T" with the palm of the other]. For some reason, a simple wordless signal is neutral enough to stop an angry barrage more effectively than words. We used this a lot when we were separated but dating and negotiating the terms of our relationship. It put a stop to blaming and non-productive inflammatory conversations; when our tempers had cooled, we could start again.*

The other important concept we learned was Green/Yellow/Red Zones ... safe and dangerous times to negotiate. We'd make a date and have an understanding of the topic to be discussed and we'd meet right after breakfast when we were fresh, optimistic and cordial from being in our Green Zones.

Over the months I mastered the art of avoiding his anger (Red Zone) but I still had stuff to learn. Barry used to get angry and fall into the Red Zone quickly especially when pressured by time or irritated by the stupidity of others who could not see his point of view. I began to see that if I was on time and even early for things, I could keep things from entering the Red Zone. Of course I used all other good communication skills and life skills to keep things from entering the Red Zone. I tried to ban the phrase "You always ... " from my vocabulary. Instead I learned to say "I don't like it when ...." I learned to ask for what I wanted rather than complaining or criticizing. I didn't react to his anger and I learned to keep a balanced view of the good and bad in life.

Over the years I had developed a very negative view of the world. Little things ... big results. I stopped trying to placate and began to deal directly with issues within the safety of Green/Yellow/Red Zone formula. We shared the ideas with family members and close friends so they could help us with anger management, better communication and understanding of our challenges. I began to announce "Red" or "Yellow Zone" to warn people when I was ripe for an angry interchange. This might occur on the golf course when I hit the ball badly, when people put women down or when I am driving. For the most part working out, yoga practice and meditation help me stay in the Green Zone where I can safely deal with most of the situations life sends my way. Learning to manage time better and having realistic expectations for myself also keep me from becoming impatient with or critical of others. Over the years Barry and I have learned to stay in the Green Zone most of the time. Now we enjoy being with each other and also with family members and friends, and we have a happy marriage, again.

Leslie

While working with Leslie and Barry, I also realized that like other couples, they had differences in communication styles. Leslie, many times, shared for the sake of sharing, while Barry was always in a problem-solving mood. When Barry offered his logical and analytical solutions, Leslie got very frustrated and slipped into the Yellow Zone. I gradually helped Leslie to announce her expectations before the dialogue. I encouraged her to say to Barry, "I don't want you to solve the problem. I just want you to listen." Such a request helped Barry to relax, take off his problem-solving hat and just listen — which was quite reassuring for Leslie. Such a request helped to keep their communication in the Green Zone.

Another crucial factor in the recovery of their relationship was the Time Out strategy. As Leslie states, the referee's hand signal used by either of the spouses during a heated discussion was sufficient to put it into a pause mode until both parties had cooled the tension they were feeling. Interestingly, I have noticed that with many couples, one partner instinctively knows that he or she needs to stop a discussion and take time to calm down their thoughts and the situation. The other may not accept this, and may follow their retreating partner around the house, continuing to talk and press home their point. Anything to win. This often results in a major blow-up, with the first partner yelling, "Leave me alone!" and the other feeling unfairly shut off from the dialogue. With such couples, I emphasize the value of honouring the request of the partner who needs time out, with the proviso that a future time will be agreed upon for the discussion to continue. In that way, the one who is upset can recover, and the other is reassured that they will have the opportunity to talk further without rancour.

Leslie and Barry made such wonderful progress in therapy that we wrote and filmed a documentary, "Growing Alone — Growing Together," in which they shared their struggles and highlighted how they transformed their Red Zone relationship into the true companionship found in the Green Zone. They have become a role model for many couples attending our clinic, who saw little hope for their failing marriages. Barry and Leslie have helped many realize that with proper professional help, couples living in the Red Zone can learn to live in the joy of the Green Zone and lead a happy and healthy married life instead of an unproductive coexistence.

BACK TOGETHER AFTER A PAINFUL SEPARATION

With couples who had serious problems and were unable to resolve their conflicts in therapy while living under the same roof, I suggested that they separate temporarily. Such a separation provides an opportunity for soul-searching that can lead to a change in their attitude toward each other. When I felt, during their separate times with me that they had reached the point in therapy where they were ready to talk together, I suggested that they meet for an hour to have a pleasant time together during which they would discuss neutral things in what I called "A Green Zone Hour." Afterwards, they went their separate ways until the next time they would be together. As they started to experience successful Green Hours, I asked them to gradually increase the Green Hour until it became two hours and then, when appropriate progress had been made, to an afternoon or morning and finally to a week-end. It was as if they were dating again to help build their relationship on a new foundation. If the couple was honest, open and sincere, in most instances they were successful in joining together again and living happily.

Ross and Kayla were one such couple. Their marriage

had teetered on the edge of the Yellow/Red line for much of their life together. Finally Ross, in his many attempts to control all aspects of their relationship, pushed his wife too far. Here he shares his observations of their journey from stormy seas to smooth sailing.

Dear Dr. Sohail

In the last year and a half, my wife and I have been through a very difficult time both emotionally and in our marital life. After twelve years together, five of them as a married couple sharing a home, we experienced a conflict that caused us to separate for a period of eight months. It was my wife's decision to leave our home and take up residence in an apartment about an hour's drive from the town in which we live. My wife Kayla did this in a spirit of affection, saying at the time she moved out that she felt it was necessary for us to improve the quality of our marriage over the long term. As you can imagine, this was still extremely difficult for me to accept. I was left asking myself what had gone wrong, and what I needed to do to reconcile with her. After seeking marriage counselling with you and your colleague, Anne Aguirre, I was introduced to the idea that people live in Green, Yellow, or Red Zones in terms of their emotional state. Along with other routes I have taken to improve my personal life and my marriage, it has proved to be a helpful concept to make us both more aware of the positives and the negatives of our day-to-day interaction with each other. I am acutely aware of the trouble many couples at our stage of life have in keeping marriages together. Two of our very close friends have had a brother and a sister who have experienced bitter break-ups in the last several months. It is my hope that this story will help other couples who are going through a similarly tough time to recognize how they can improve their relationships before marital disharmony occurs.

I work as a high school teacher and originally sought psychotherapy because of a problem that I faced in my employment. The stresses on me throughout my eleven years of teaching have been very high, and I found that I had become used to a routine that permitted me only to receive about four hours of sleep a night. This pattern did not cause me a great deal of physical illness, as I was still quite young and only at the beginning of my career. I was unaware, however, that my lifestyle was creating a pattern of unhealthy emotional stress that was soon to take a heavy toll on my marriage. As I later discovered, my life had been constantly in the Yellow Zone described by you during the months of the year when I was busy preparing for and teaching my classes. This meant that I was in a continual rush, on edge, feeling anxious rather than calm, relaxed and comfortable, and suffering from tension due to the habit of functioning for weeks at a time on so little sleep.

While my wife and I had what I would describe as a very happy marriage, problems began to surface even in our first year of marriage that resulted from my inability to see the danger signs of stress affecting my emotional well-being. Exhausted from my week of work when the weekends came along, I found myself getting irritated by small matters much more easily than I would if I were in a normal, well-rested state of mind. I found it difficult to control my temper at times, and would have outbursts of anger that caused me to act in inappropriate ways towards my wife in order to resolve conflicts we had over various matters. I once threw a shoe at the wall in anger. On one occasion I even threw a cake she had baked across the floor to show her my displeasure. This was very immature and aggressive behaviour, and I was taking great risks with something very precious to me, my marital relationship. I now recognize these incidents as cases of my slipping from the Yellow Zone into the Red Zone, but at the time I always felt justified in doing so because I believed the onus was on my wife to be more sensitive and respectful of my wishes. I always felt extremely guilty for these outbursts and would profusely apologize to her afterwards, but the pattern did not change. Oddly enough, I did not have trouble with disagreements in my married life during times when I was not busy at school, such as the summer holidays. This was because I was able to stay in what you called the Green Zone, as my sleeping patterns had returned to normal. It was not difficult for me to remain patient and calm, and avoid the emotional strain of marital discord when I was not on edge due to the pressures of my work.

The entire situation came to a head in the fall of 1999, when my wife and I began to have increasing tension between us over financial issues and over who should be the one to take responsibility for different domestic tasks. This is what I have come to understand as our differing view of our domestic-economic situation. While my wife works her income is lower than mine and I had great difficulty accepting her demand that I place no expectations on her in terms of domestic support around the house. She resented being required to earn her keep as though she was in a subservient role. To my mind this seemed only a fair expectation. To her, this was exploitation.

During one extremely heated argument, I allowed my feelings of anger to get the best of me and I struck my wife. With the support of her family, she decided that evening that the issues were severe enough and my behaviour was inappropriate enough to warrant a temporary separation. My sessions with you and Anne Aguirre became concerned, not only with my sleeping patterns, but also with my marital relationship. Kayla agreed to attend the sessions along with me, and we began the long process of repairing the damage that I had created in both of our lives. In retrospect, I am incredibly grateful to my wife for having the tenacity to seek what was best for the two us, and to show the commitment to our marriage that allowed us to make it through this difficult time. Without her desire to make our marriage better with this separation and her willingness to seek help as well, we might not have been able to save our marriage. This remains true, despite the fact that I felt, apart from my occasional problems controlling my temper, that I had cared for her needs and sought her fulfillment in life as a good husband should do.

Despite the best of intentions on my part, the positive interactions on which good relationships depend can be irreparably damaged by just a few Red Zone situations where emotional strain is allowed to slip completely out of control. I paid a heavy price for my reckless behaviour, and needed the help of a professional to gradually change my way of behaving so I could focus on my own well-being as well as the foundation of my family's comfort.

I am very ashamed of my behaviour towards my wife, the one person in my life whom I love the most and with whom I share the closest of relationships. While my attitude about male/female relationships needed to be adjusted subsequent to our break-up, I feel that a similar problem in another marriage might not have become so heated if the problem of Red Zone emotional states had not been my personal cross to bear.

Learning to constantly monitor myself in terms of Green, Yellow and Red Zones has been helpful to me personally in overcoming my tendency to spike up into erratic emotional states. If I feel an argument coming on between Kayla and myself, I recognize the Yellow Zone and disengage from the conflict until such time as I have returned to the Green Zone and can take up the issue with her calmly and rationally.

This process of calming the situation down can sometimes be accomplished in a few minutes, but sometimes it takes as long as an entire day. The important rule to remember is to avoid engaging in a discussion about any issue of conflict unless both parties are ready and able to enter into a conflict resolution interaction that will be mature and successful. It was a revelation to me to read books during the summer holidays that addressed the whole issue of conflict in families. It taught me techniques to resolve such conflicts based on a policy of maturity, consensus and mutual respect, and by avoiding verbal and physical below-the-belt abuses which are so destructive to intimate relationships.

Perhaps most importantly, the whole experience has had a positive impact on my own state of health, as I am gradually learning to be aware of the lifestyle habits that set me up for emotional strain in the first place. I am not completely free of the concern that similar trouble may surface again in the future, but I am doing the best I can to learn from my mistakes. What I am cautiously pleased to be able to report is that my happy married life has been restored for the better part of another school year now, and there have been no more incidents of violence or anger out of control. Even on the level of our emotional interaction, I have been very careful not to enter into the Yellow Zone whenever I sense it beginning, to better manage the tone of the interaction taking place in our home.

Many would say that I am extremely fortunate to have been able to make things right with Kayla. I feel that without her loving support during such a difficult time, and without the availability of professional help such as that provided by you and Anne Aguirre, I would be writing a different story.

Ross

Ross makes a brief mention of a very significant issue in the couple's relationship, which I often see in my work. It is the issue of finances, and in particular the matter of how much each partner should contribute to the household and how the money should be spent. Although Ross had a far higher income than his wife, he felt that she should contribute equally to the household budget. Failing that, he thought she should make up for her smaller contribution by doing extra housework. Either way his position made his wife feel pressured: to come home after her stressful day at work and start in on a schedule of domestic activity around the home, or to match his financial contribution and have little spending money left for herself. Additionally, Ross exercised tight control over the couple's spending, even though they were very secure financially.

I discussed with them my concept of the Love Model and the Business Model of relationships. In the Business Model, the focus is on financial contributions and the relationship, although important, is secondary. The goals are fairness and justice, and in such relationships it is acceptable to keep a record of all the contributions by the parties involved. By contrast, in the Love Model the relationship is primary and the goal is that each partner should feel comfortable and secure. Each contributes what they can freely and spontaneously, without a ledger being kept or any pressure exerted to ensure compliance.

I shared with Ross that relationships between friends, lovers and spouses flourish only in the Love Model. As Ross learned to change his attitude and began to practise the Love Model, his relationship with Kayla improved and he learned to give and take money and affection freely. Although the couple had work to do on other aspects of their marriage, the resolution of the financial struggle was a major step in bringing their relationship out of the Red Zone into the happiness available to them when they choose to live in the Green Zone.

DISSOLVING YOUR INTIMATE RELATIONSHIP

Although I try my best to help couples resolve their conflicts and recover their happiness in their Green Zones, there are times when after months of therapy, I realize that irreversible damage has been done to the relationship. In many of these cases, the spouses become so angry, resentful and deeply bitter that their conflicts cannot be resolved. When that time is at hand, I ask that they consider dissolving the marriage and to try to live in the Green Zone on their own, hoping that their next relationship will be better than the last one. Such a transformation is easier when the couple does not have children.

One such couple was Bill and Jennifer. After the relationship dissolved, Jennifer stopped coming but Bill stayed with his individual and group therapy. He made such a profound change in his personality and lifestyle that not only did he learn to live in the Green Zone by himself but within a year started a new loving relationship that lives in the Green Zone. Other group members are quite impressed by his progress. He shares his story with us.

Dear Dr. Sohail

I became introduced to your concept of the Green, Yellow and Red Zones as a means of understanding others and my emotional and rational state of interactions. This concept has proven useful in regulating my temperament and responses in both my personal and professional life. It is often said that the beginning of New Years is a time of reflection and resolution. So it only seems fitting that I write this letter today. My reflective journey takes me back some 11 years when I met my wife and was struck with her sensitivity, playfulness, innocence and beauty. I quickly fell in love and enjoyed her spirit for life but I struggled with her insecurities that she brought into the relationship. All for good reason, given the trials of her upbringing.

As our relationship progressed, her insecurities became apparent as I began to find myself assuming the majority of responsibility for decisions made in the marriage with regards to personal, financial, social and family matters. As I reflect, I see how damaging this was for the relationship and me. I soon began to feel under pressure to perform perfectly, without fault for she seemed to adore the abilities I had to plan, organize and remember details, all the while with an outgoing personality. Gradually, her admiration turned to suspicion and accusations, I began to become anxious and at times depressed. Some would say I lived in the Yellow Zone. I felt responsible for the mundane expectations of life, for the well-being of our relationship and her emotional wellness. You can well imagine that over an extended period of time I failed at this, the pressure slowly pushed me to becoming emotionally distant. I began to feel that my life, spirit and feelings had been under scrutiny to the point of becoming flat.

The business of day-to-day life seemed to sustain the relationship but it did not help it to grow. There was many a time that my outgoing manner compromised the trust in the relationship as I struggled with her personal belief that I was unfaithful. This personal assault was attacking my worthiness and dismissing my commitment and love for her. Living in the Yellow Zone, I began to feel the need to justify my actions and existence to circumvent the next accusations; this did not help with the communication and intimacy in the marriage. However, it must be said that before Yellow there was Green. We experienced some great joys and laughter and overcame some trying times. We truly could support each other, the illness of her father, the separation and reunification of my parents' marriage. My wife and I had the strength to stay supportive and united for the sake of others.

The marriage continued for nine and a half years through the decision not to have children due to family mental illness, two homes, job instability and changes, and increased financial stability. We seemed to weather these changes but at times only while in the Red Zone. Communication and intimacy became lost souls in the marriage. I gradually found myself with little emotional energy, most often angry about feeling so responsible and then accused. I felt defeated and we attended couple-counselling at the clinic. I began to take antidepressants and you worked with us on communicating our needs and balancing our lives. However, it was too late, my wife announced unexpectedly that she was leaving the marriage, not only was I completely devastated, it was equally shocking to others in our public lives.

My Red Zone went into full alert; I began to feel incredible responsibility for the failure of the marriage, for my own failure as a husband and plans that were rampant. Excessive drinking became a daily occurrence. My life ran completely out of control, I feared for myself, I feared that her perception of me was accurate. The Red Zone lingered for months, the loss of a wife, marriage, in-laws, mutual friends, the judgement of others and emotional attacks were so overwhelming. Recovery had to begin and this is where the resolutions have become important.

Today, I live mostly in the Green Zone with the occasional trip to the Yellow Zone. It is nice to experience life in a way that the world is generally a kind and happy place. People for the most part have good intentions and are well meaning. I did not happen to return to this place in my life by chance. People would say that time heals, it is with this that I disagree. I believe that time will give you distance from the problem but that it is the "doing" that heals. So I gradually gained strength to take some healing steps, first it was to stay connected to God and the church, to begin each day with prayer and include it in the ongoing events of each day. Secondly, it was to welcome support of family, allow them to love me and hold me when I was most vulnerable; it is rare to feel such unconditional love and yet I was blessed to have such family support.

The mystery of other friendships is amazing. They gave me the gift of support and perspective without accusation and blame. These are the people that are not born to your family but become a part of your family. Recovery was also aided by my weekly journal for my "Vision to Reality," as introduced to me by a dear friend, who saw my strength to succeed and offered me a personal resource to harvest this strength and put it to positive use. This tool helped me to be grounded in the state I wanted to obtain and was able to allow the focus to be on health versus hell.

Self-discovery was essential to my return to the Green Zone and this was created by my continued attendance at the clinic, taking the antidepressants with the benefits of feeling less burdened. I have attended three separate support systems all at different Zones. They all have had a profound effect on my healing. I believe they have supported me and challenged me to accept and dispel the vicious cycle of responsibility I was in. Now is the time to recognize others' and my Zones and to continue to focus on recovery and restraint from the invitation and reactions of the Yellow and Red Zones.

It is possible to enjoy life after crisis. It takes openness to accept the support of others, and to have personal perseverance and determination. During the crisis you question its benefits, for I am thankful for my marriage and the gifts learned and received. Given this experience, I have grown into a "Better Man" (a song that I listened to many a time while I was in the Red Zone). I thank my ex-wife for the experience and wish her as much growth in her recovery. To this day the divorce would seem more damaging to the marriage, than the marriage itself. Dr. Sohail, you say, and I believe that, "What you can't resolve you then dissolve."

Thanks to all who have participated, contributed, and walked with me during the journey. A special blessing to the new angel in my life, love is possible again.

Bill

Part Three

GREEN YELLOW RED ZONE

SYSTEMS

GREEN YELLOW RED ZONE SYSTEMS

Once people recognize their emotional zones and are aware of the quality of their intimate relationships, I encourage them to recognize the systems they live in. Most people live in numerous systems simultaneously:

Family System
Work System
Social/Community System

I share with people that, like individuals and relationships, human systems also have an individual character and that systems also live in different Zones. Recognizing the Zones of the Systems and one's relationship within them is very important in recognizing the changes in one's emotional Zones. Systems have a major impact on individuals. In most cases systems are more powerful than individuals.

FAMILY ZONES

We are all part of a family system as we are growing up and most of us get married and have a family we call our own. Lucky are those who grow up in a healthy Green Zone family and are nurtured by their parents. Growing up in a Green Zone family ensures a confident personality with positive self-image, self-worth, and self-confidence. In Green Zone families, people have positive role models and are more likely to have Green Zone relationships in the future.

People who grow up in Yellow Zone and Red Zone families are unfortunate. They have to face tension, anxiety and poor communication in their various environments. People who grow up in the Yellow Zone are chronically anxious, frustrated, angry or sad. They might have managed to acquire a family, a job and even a social circle of acquaintances, but they lack a general attitude of happiness. It is not uncommon for them to visit the Red Zone by having panic attacks, losing control and having fights with their loved ones — or getting so depressed as to be admitted to the hospital for short periods. When they continue to exist in the Red Zone, and do not get proper help to deal with the issue or issues which send them there, they get stuck in the Red Zone and are unable to exit it using their free will.

A woman I counseled had struggled for years with panic attacks, the origins of which she traced back to her childhood of a life lived in a perpetual Yellow Zone family. Natalie was a bright and competent nurse who, despite her sometimes incapacitating illness, was pursuing a successful career as well as caring for her three children.

Following hospitalization for acute anxiety, she was referred to me for further assistance. As is my practice, I met with her and her husband to discuss the situation and arrange a plan of care. Natalie started to come for individual, marital and group therapy sessions as an outpatient, and a nurse visited her home regularly to offer support and suggestions. Gradually Natalie improved and recovered, although it was a slow and intensive process. Since Natalie had never lived in the Green Zone, it was difficult for her to differentiate between these two lifestyles, healthy from unhealthy, and mature from immature. She continues to struggle, but over the years she has grown out of her Red Zone into the Yellow Zone and has finally achieved a good life in the newness of her Green Zone. I asked her to share her story.

Dr. Sohail

I grew up in the Yellow Zone and led a very anxious life. I had panic attacks most of my adult life. My earliest memory of a panic attack was when I was a young teenager. It was at a church youth group when we were practising for a concert. I became terrified that I would make a fool of myself and have to leave the room. I had many such attacks as a teenager, some in social functions, some at school. My family was quite aware of what was occurring as both my parents and two of my three sisters have them also. I remember a very loving upbringing but one with high expectations and a lot of criticism. I understand now that a lot of my panic stems from what I learned from my mother through observation and the spoken word. Though I always felt loved I was constantly criticized. I often felt nothing I did was right. My mother constantly talked about the way things had to be for her or she couldn't cope. She was very controlling. By the time I left home for nursing school, I felt I had never made any decisions on my own. Thinking back now, most of my panic centered around feelings of inferiority and terror of embarrassing myself in public.

On to Nursing School

Many times during change of shift at report time or in classes I'd feel trapped and wanted to leave. At my nursing graduation, I remember being so panicky that it was a nightmare getting through it.

Then I went to Texas for my first job, and I wasn't sure I was going to be able to get on the plane. In Texas I had my first opportunity to work with a psychiatrist about the panic attacks though we didn't accomplish much as shortly afterward I returned home. By this time I was functioning reasonably well. I was able to work and handle many social situations.

Shortly after returning home, I got engaged to be married. The number of panic attacks increased as I had no confidence in my decision and I was afraid Jonathan would reject me if he knew I had panic attacks. For some time I felt my panic was an indication that there was something mentally wrong with me, something to be greatly ashamed about and to be hidden at all cost. Prior to the wedding, my nerves as we called it at that time, were so bad that I tried another psychiatrist. The experience was a disaster. Some of the things he said to me were humiliating in the extreme.

After I married Jonathan, I tried a psychologist. At this point I really wanted to get over these attacks, as I was afraid I'd pass them onto my children. To me that would be the worst thing possible. Initially it went well, but then my psychologist left the hospital where she was working and went into private practice. The sessions were not covered by OHIP. Jonathan ended up pressuring me to stop them due to the cost. Most of the sessions went over the origin of my illness and very little on getting over them. At least I developed a little understanding if not acceptance. At this point I started to understand how my upbringing contributed to my panic attacks and became quite angry with my mother, but unable to express my anger to her. At this point work was hard. I was tired a lot and a number of social things were very stressful. As we were so anxious about money, this built up to me being terrified of even going out to dinner with Jonathan as I was afraid I'd have a panic attack and have to leave therefore spoiling the evening and wasting our money. Jonathan was very preoccupied with money in our earlier years of marriage.

Falling Into the Red Zone

Things got worse after the children were born. All of them had asthma (which kept me up every night for months in a row over six years). There were other stresses. Major surgery in the family, constant school difficulties and my father's illness and death. Jonathan became very withdrawn and dumped the whole workload on me. He constantly compared me to his mother saying that she did everything and so should I, as I was not working outside the home. He felt his sole responsibility should be to go to work. I was living in the Red Zone all the time. Sleeping little, often unable to eat, vomited often when anxiety was high and lost about 15 pounds. I had panic attacks daily and the rest of the time felt panicky and exhausted.

Nights were usually the worst. There was a lot of resentment between Jonathan and me. I resented him because he would not help (I had to deal with more than his mother ever had to) and Jonathan resented me because he did not feel he should have to help me. His idea was that since he brought in the money I should handle the home and the kids. He was very uptight about money. He refused to pay for any help. We went to Florida once and I had a panic attack so bad that I had to go to see a psychiatrist and he told me to go back home and be admitted to the hospital. I tried again to get professional help at a hospital in Scarborough but I was made to feel so defective that I did not stay. Eventually I collapsed at my family doctor's office who then hospitalized me which confirmed to me that I had a mental illness.

While I was hospitalized Jonathan paid for his

mother to fly in and take care of the kids. When I was let out on a day pass she said she could not share the house with me. I either had to leave or she would. She then encouraged Jonathan to hide the car so I would not take it and convinced him that I was a mental case and that he could sue for custody of the children and win and she would move in and raise them as long as he got rid of me. At that point I was sent to the psychiatric hospital to be admitted and I met you in the admitting department. You convinced Jonathan to ask his mom to leave and to take me back home and get help.

Recovering to the Yellow Zone with Therapy

I started seeing you on a regular basis. In the hospital there was also a crisis line, so if I needed help at night, I could talk to the nurses. I also saw a nurse who came to my home every week to offer support. You also convinced Jonathan to hire a housekeeper until I got better. I was terrified of collapsing again and being put back in the hospital and end up losing my kids to my mother-in-law. I had a lot of anger towards my husband for his criticism and lack of support as well as my family who seemed unable to do anything either. With your encouragement I started to feel better. At that time Jonathan decided to get a new job and move. I did not want to loose all my support so we talked about divorce. I felt he was selfish thinking only of his needs and never of anyone else's. It was probably his way of coping at the time but I did not know that and it did not help our children or me. In therapy, Jonathan was convinced not to move.

It ended up taking at least three years of individual, group and martial therapy for me to start moving out of living in the Red Zone all the time. Gradually I started spending more time in the Yellow, than in the Red. One of the things that was hard for me to learn was that Jonathan wasn't coping. It took me a long time to understand that he was completely withdrawn from the family (his attempt to cope) which is why he was unable to help me and why he was angry when I would not do it all. It took me a long time to get over my resentment for Jonathan. I moved from the Red Zone to the Yellow Zone by consistently doing two things:

1) *Replacing panic thoughts with distractions and therefore thinking less about panic. I started with concentrating when I was reading and watching TV. I also planned teaching sessions for Scouts. Since it took a lot of time for the research, it was most successful.*
2) *Concentrating on pretending to be happy even when I felt my worst. Eventually pretending became reality.*

Growing Into the Green Zone

After living in the Yellow Zone for nearly five years, I am learning to visit the Green Zone and hopefully to live there one day. I am trying to get over the terror of having panic attacks and the feelings of shame and inferiority that I have about myself because of the panic. In the last five years I had only one or two panic attacks a year. I can work and take care of myself now. My marriage is much better. I can see slow but definite progress. I never have panic attacks at work or at home, only in extremely stressful social situations. Now I do not avoid situations because of the fear of panic attacks. I like myself more and am developing more self-confidence.

I am also getting a better understanding of my feelings about my mother. Even though I still feel that she was a major factor in my developing panic attacks in the first place, I now believe that her rigid control was her attempt to control her own panic attacks. I believe she was afraid that if everything was not just a certain way she would loose control of herself. Now I feel that no matter what I learned as a child, it is now my choice to stay the same or change it. It is no longer my mother's fault. I can't change her. I wish I could encourage her to get help. Life would be easier for her if she received help but she would not consider it and that is her choice too. For me to stay in the Green Zone I would like to:

> *Not fear panic attacks,*
> *Improve my opinion of myself,*
> *Reduce anxiety in some social situations and interpersonal relations.*

I am now spending more and more time in the Green Zone, and feeling its happiness for the first time in my life.

Natalie

Natalie's story clearly highlights that psychotherapy can help people transform their lifestyles so they can live in the Green Zone even if they have never experienced it before. A crisis in life is a mixed blessing; with proper support and professional help a breakdown can be transformed into a breakthrough.

Along with those who grew up in Yellow Zone families, I also met others who spent their lives in the Green Zone but because of serious crises in their lives, fell into disarray, lost their grip on happiness, and fell through the Yellow Zone into the Red. It was quite a scary experience for them. When the crisis lasted more than a few months, they became tired and exhausted and started to feel hopeless and ended being too helpless to help themselves find the path of recovery. They became afraid they might never return to live in the Green Zone. One such case was Diana who experienced a major crisis when her daughter became depressed and suicidal. It was difficult to convince Diana that since she had lived in the Green Zone most of her life, it would be easier for her to return to the Green Zone than for those who had never experienced it. She shares her story with us.

Dr. Sohail

I grew up in the Green Zone and lived in it for most of the forty-six years of my life. I was a happy kid, a very fortunate teenager from a middle-upper class family in a small town just outside of Toronto. Of course, we only realize this in retrospect because we rarely appreciate what we have until it's gone or behind us. I probably had some bad times when I was a teenager in the 1960s and 1970s but I remember the good times. We travelled quite a bit with a trailer and as a family we shared a lot of holidays, camping and sightseeing. I have two older brothers, and was especially close to my brother who was just two years older. I was part of the school choir, in drama, in a literature group, enjoyed music and hung out with all kinds of people — geeks, hippies, and everything in between. I was very independent, I went horseback riding by myself in three different places around my hometown that I could reach by bike. I often went to a conservation area and just played my guitar by the river and enjoyed writing songs. I enjoyed nature at an early age and find now it is all I really want — a walk in the woods to re-energize and rejuvenate my spirit in nature. I treasure the memories of riding about the whole day through the valleys and hilltops with no fear or ill thoughts, just me and my horse. I biked everywhere until I could drive around town and into the city where I really enjoyed theatre and the galleries. Going to coffee houses and seeing Bruce Cockburn, Joni Mitchell and Murray McLaughlin, all starting out in their careers are some of my fondest memories of time in the big city. It really dates me but they are still around and playing their music. It's quite incredible, really. I feel very lucky coming from those awesome times that I grew up in as a teen.

Woodstock, outside concerts, huge Chicago concerts, music was big time. Crime was not profuse, you could walk anywhere at night basically, in the city too, without fear and life was pretty good. Who watched the news? I was pretty oblivious to what was happening in the world. Who had heard of murder in Toronto? The news just wasn't something we paid attention to. The only thing I can remember being afraid of was drugs. I didn't get into drugs at all, so I consider when I look back that I had good common sense, and a lot of free-

dom to explore what I needed and wanted without barriers. I may not have had the nurturing conversation and friendship with my parents — but they let me be. I had lots of friends, enjoyed my own company and lived in the Green Zone.

I would have to say that I was enthusiastic about the good things in life and chose to be happy and tried new things, to experience all that I could. People told me that I was cheerful, always willing to lend a hand and nice to be around. That seemed to separate me from a lot of people I knew. Some kids had to work and I knew several who got pregnant, some that did drugs and had real problems. Remembering that now, I felt sorry for them but their problems weren't my problems. There was always something to do, something new to learn and I carried that through six different jobs, from working with students at a university, to editing a newspaper, public relations, and then I became an independent contractor. I think as I look back, I was very proud of my accomplishments because I excelled at what I did. I gave it 100% plus, and if something didn't pan out, I moved on. I allowed myself that freedom. I always went for a job that was challenging, fun and paid enough to get by. I'm not a conceited person at all. I am very down to earth, fun loving, a traveler, an outdoor enthusiast and an artist at heart. I compose music and love to play it. Basically I like myself and I thought for the most part I was a good mom, wife, sister and daughter. I was liked by most people and I liked most people so what was so bad about life?

Falling Into the Red Zone

Well, it happened very suddenly. My daughter went into a major crisis. She was sixteen and there were signs that she was depressed. Being a sensitive teen, she over-reacted to life in general. I took her to a doctor and she prescribed anti-depressants in the fall of 1997. We talked a lot. We always had conversations about everything and I felt I had knowledge of what she was going through. She had always asked about what it was like when I grew up and of course I told her all the good things. Thinking I was doing the right thing by answering her questions openly and honestly proved me wrong big time. She wanted the same thing. She could not understand a lot of the horrible things she saw on TV. She could not grasp why kids were so cruel and nasty to her and others. Most girls it seemed to her were bitches and guys were just after one thing. It was not like that in my teen years. She is very pretty and smart and I thought that she might be intimidating people.

She had been cutting her wrists, without my knowledge, and was bruised in a lot of places I could not see. She was hiding her pain very well and I felt awful because I could not see it coming. She had always been a bit temperamental and spoke what she thought, but I was not hearing outlandish thoughts, or major confusion. I thought she was frustrated and making a desperate attempt to understand the world around her. She told us when she was three that she chose us as her parents. This is something, for some reason, I thought a lot about.

The night she went into crisis happened after the principal called and said she was suspended from school for three days because of her behaviour. She started hitting herself and repeatedly said she hated herself. She ended up being removed from our house by the police in handcuffs because she could not control herself, and we could not control the situation. She was taken to the hospital and put into a crisis twenty-four - hour lockup facility. She was 16 but she was with adults who were psychotic. I felt sick. As a parent you feel at such a deep level of emotion, you cannot think straight. The first thing we asked ourselves was, "What did we do wrong?" My husband and I went back over our lives. We thought we were really good parents but that everyone makes mistakes. I started to blame myself as a parent. I thought I must have done something wrong as a mother. I thought all the good things I had experienced as a teenager she could not. I thought it must be a torture for her to realize she would never have them.

My Green Zone dissolved very quickly with the realization that she needed help and we had to wait for everything as mental health services for teenagers were scarce. There were waiting lists for months. In the meanwhile she kept trying to kill herself. She overdosed on medications. She smoked dope while on her medications. She drank beer and slit her wrists. She became violent towards me when I tried to stop her from stabbing herself. My dream of a happy family life turned into a nightmare. It was a big reality bite that hurt me very deeply, and through many, many layers. She was very intelligent and philosophical but I realized I did not know my own daughter as well as I thought. My relationship with her was in the Yellow Zone for a while and then fell into the Red Zone. I started working less and less to stay home and protect my daughter from herself.

Doctors said she suffered from mood disorder and personality disorder. One psychiatrist told us that she was the most complex person he had met in his forty years of practice. He told us we were not responsible for her behaviour. She remained an outpatient for two years but was still suicidal. It is hard to live with a suicidal person for two years. It was her problem but I felt responsible for her problem for a long, long time. I was her mom and I had to look after her. I read dozens of books about mental illness, drugs, and human psychology, but only became more and more confused. It was frustrating. I had a lot of questions but very few answers.

She started to blame her father and I felt sorry for him. She became angry with her father, with God and the whole world.

While looking after her for two years, I suppressed my own feelings and did not look after my own needs. As I descended into the Red Zone I started losing my voice. I could not talk. I just whispered, sometimes I could not even do that. I stopped working and could not visit my friends. I had no voice left even to make phone calls. I felt very lonely, angry, frustrated, helpless and scared. I believed I would never get back to who I was. I was changed forever.

Recovery to the Green Zone

Finally I saw a therapist for myself. I was told I did not know my boundaries. I had gone too far. My therapist told me to cry as I had lost all track of feelings. For a while I read about divine intervention, echoes of our souls, believed in reincarnation, prayed and practised yoga. I was afraid of how I was going to live without a proper voice.

Gradually I learned in therapy that I had to disconnect emotionally from my daughter to heal myself. I had become over-involved with her mentally. With a lot of professional help I have finally achieved disconnection from my daughter. I keep my distance and do not let her control me. She is still demanding but I tell her I did all I could do. Now she has to learn to help herself. Gradually I climbed back to the Yellow Zone and when she went to the treatment center for a few weeks to deal with her depression, I climbed to the Green Zone. I just hope that I can stick to my Green Zone. I am planning to go on a trip to visit my friend in California for a few weeks by myself. I never thought I could ever do that. Now I do not let my daughter push me or suck me down into her Red Zone. I will always be there for my daughter in my Green Zone. She can drop in anytime.

Diana

WORK ZONES

Many people, besides being part of a Family System are also part of a Work System. It is important for people to recognize the Zone the Work System moves in. A Work System in the Green Zone has a fair and just environment where people feel appreciated and their concerns are taken seriously. In Yellow and Red Zones, people feel like robots. Decisions are made for political and economic reasons. There is, too often, a dehumanizing atmosphere. The communication between workers and management often breaks down and conflicts are not resolved.

Many workplaces, which started out in the Green Zone, have transformed over the years due to political and economic changes, and their work environments have gradually regressed so that the atmosphere has become a Yellow or Red Zone. We work with people who, despite staff cuts resulting in increased work loads, arbitrary transfers, and imposition of new technology without adequate training, keep working as they try to make up for the shortcomings of the workplace. Many have become increasingly frustrated and angry, feeling unenthusiastic and burnt out. It is very important to recognize that while Work Systems change, people also change over a period of time. So the dynamic relationship between people and their Work System has changed dramatically over the decades. Unfortunately many Green Work Zones have regressed to Red Work Zones. People working in such Red Zones suffer in varying degrees.

One such example was Harry. This talented teacher, who had always loved his job and looked forward to going to work, started to dread even the thought of it. I asked him to share his story.

Dr. Sohail

I have been a High School teacher for 26 years, with extensive teaching experience in Sciences, Mathematics, Technology, Guidance and Work experience programs. Fifteen years ago I was appointed to co-ordinate the co-operative education program at my school. Within three years I succeeded in increasing the student enrolment in the program by five hundred percent. As a result of this rapid growth, additional teaching staff was needed to help with the program.

Unfortunately, few knowledgeable or dedicated teachers were assigned to me by the administration, especially during the early years. Every year, as teachers' timetables were being assigned, I pleaded with the administration to provide me with appropriate staff. I pointed out some deficiencies in the work ethic of some of those assigned to the co-op department. (I had received numerous complaints from students who were infrequently visited at their work placements, from parents whose children were misplaced and neglected, and from employers who were not adequately served.) Despite all the reasons and evidence given, my pleas for help fell on deaf ears. In fact, I was criticized by the newly-appointed principal of the school, when I made him aware of these deficiencies (criticizing one's colleagues is a taboo in education, no matter how incompetent they are).

Shortly thereafter, another extremely incompetent person (with political connections) was appointed to head the co-operative education program. I couldn't believe the unfairness, hypocrisy and betrayal I felt. I became disillusioned and angry with the entire educational system. Yet I remained in the co-operative education program, essentially managing the whole program as before.

The newly appointed coordinator lacked interpersonal and management skills necessary for the community-based work experience programs. The complaints kept arriving almost daily. As someone who had worked hard to build the co-operative education program, I felt compelled to maintain the integrity of the program and to make it work at any cost. I could not allow our students to be rejected, misplaced or neglected by the inexperienced and uncommitted co-op teachers. I continued to struggle on my own, managing more, way more than my maximum allowed number of students. I routinely screened, interviewed, counseled, placed and supervised in various work settings nearly 200 very diverse students each year. The workload was grueling. I frequently missed lunch breaks, and regularly delayed visits to the rest room. Though often exhausted and even physically ill, I continued to carry on with the relentless pace, seldom missing a day of work.

Eventually, my physical and emotional health began to deteriorate; I began to depend on laxatives, decongestants, and in ever-increasing quantities, alcohol. I frequently required medical treatment for abdominal and respiratory disorders, and have over the years undergone many medical tests and procedures. I experienced countless sinus and respiratory infections, and had to use decongestants virtually every working day. I had difficulty sleeping, regularly getting up every hour during the night, writing reminder notes to myself, wide awake, ready to go to work at four or five a.m. I began to experience shortness of breath and irregular heartbeats. I began to consume alcohol in ever-increasing quantities.

Recently, the work environment had deteriorated to an all time low. It was becoming even more poisoned, both physically as well as socially. My physical and emotional health had reached rock bottom. Physically and emotionally exhausted, I no longer looked forward to the job I used to love. I have experienced frequent mood swings for many years, often feeling tense, angry and sad. Angry and disillusioned with the current crisis in education, I began to detest the people who use it for political gain, and refused to network with those teachers who have betrayed others for personal gain.

I began having difficulty relating to some of my long-time friends, and chose to no longer associate with many. I found their company uninteresting or unnecessary. I began to avoid social gatherings, and lost interest in many of the activities I once enjoyed. I withdrew from the outside world, and tended more and more to do things alone. My home became my refuge, a bottle of wine my best friend. I was utterly miserable.

My greatest source of pain and sadness, however, has been my failing relationship with my family. Over the last few years, the relationship with my wife and daughters has become strained and at times completely dysfunctional. I frequently found their conduct lacking or objectionable. This has been a source of much discord and unhappiness in our home. The communication with my daughters has become strained and infrequent. They started avoiding me, and sought guidance from their mother or their friends.

I have, it seems, succeeded in driving the most important people in my life away from me. This, without a doubt, has been my life's greatest failure, which causes me enormous anguish and despair. At times I feel that my life is a colossal mistake, and believe that they would all be better off without me. Many times in recent years, I wished I could just go to sleep and never wake up again. I became unafraid of death, and often thought about it as an escape from the nightmare I was living. Many times I contemplated ending it all on my own. My life had no meaning.

Yet for some reason I carried on. My work, though stressful, kept me distracted from myself. My students' success continued to be of importance to me, and their appreciation for my guidance continued to be one of the few bright spots in my life. But I was only existing, and at the back of my mind I felt that my work was only delaying what I thought was inevitable.

In February I became afflicted with Bell's palsy (a

painful neurological paralysis of the face), which according to the neurologist, may be caused by stress and stress-related weakening of the immune system. Since September, I have also had four respiratory infections, which I believe were caused by the dirty work environment. My surgeon is also of the opinion that my bowel disorders are directly related to the stress of my job. Yet if it was not for the Bell's Palsy, I would have probably continued to go to work — dirt, stress, resentment, anger and all.

I have visited my place of work on two occasions during the last three months. Not much has changed there. The place is still filthy and overcrowded. The ventilation system in the school is antiquated and inadequate. My office, like the rest of the school, is infrequently cleaned due to the cutbacks in custodial staff. Teacher morale is depressingly low. Within minutes of my arrival, my sinuses become congested, and my abdominal muscles tighten up. I feel uneasy and anxious to get out of there as soon as possible. (Since the beginning of my medical leave, those were the only two days when my bowels failed to function normally.)

Once this school was a place of great fun, enjoyment and pride for me. That, however, has all changed. There is no longer any doubt in my mind that I have compromised my health there over the years, and that returning to work there would be detrimental to my well being, and my relationship with my family. That, I am no longer willing to do.

Since my leave from work, my physical and to some extent emotional well-being have improved. By mid-

April I began to feel better. I was beginning to feel more energetic, and less anxious and tense. I felt it was time for me to get involved in some voluntary work in my community. I have for several years worked as an occasional volunteer for the local soup kitchen. This time I wanted to try something different. After a few inquiries and an interview, I became a volunteer driver with the local community care agency. Several times each week I transport, elderly and infirm clients for their medical appointments at hospitals and clinics using my car.

I have met some very diverse and interesting people, whose experiences and lives lived are often quite unique and amazing. Their illness and infirmity are usually apparent, and probably treatable with medications or therapy. However, it is quite often their loneliness which seems to be breaking their spirit and their will to live better. I am convinced that in many of these cases, it is their loneliness which is the underlying cause of some of their illnesses. This neglect of our elderly is truly tragic, and needs to be brought into the open.

Despite an occasional downer, I have found it most uplifting and satisfying helping these folks. Over time, I have gotten to know many of them quite well, and have become their favourite driver. I occasionally take them to the donut shop and listen to their life stories over a cup of coffee or tea. Their stories, which are sometimes full of sadness and tragedy, have forced me to look at my own life in a more positive way.

Harry

In the last few years I have met more and more people who have suffered because of their toxic work environment. It seems as if the institutions, be they schools, banks or hospitals, are transforming into Red Zones. The bureaucracies have not been sensitive to people's needs. The prejudices and injustices are increasing to dehumanizing proportions. Even in our practice, we are seeing more and more people who are breaking down at work and going on stress-related leaves and living on long-term disability payments. I am convinced that their disabilities are far more emotional than physical. It is becoming an epidemic. It is very difficult for people to live in a Green Zone emotionally when they are exposed daily to such a negative Red Zone environment. As Harry noted, the unfortunate fallout from the Red Work Zone is the toll that it also takes on family and social life.

It is also significant that those who have an idealistic and perfectionistic personality, and who have high expectations of themselves and others, suffer far more than those around them in the same workplace who can be more indifferent to the situation. I encourage them to lower their expectations or seek another work environment where they are more compatible with their surrounding. They may have difficulty abandoning a work situation in which they have invested their integrity and where they truly care how the organization is treating its clients. They seem willing to sacrifice themselves to provide the level of service that they believe the company or agency should offer, all the time hoping that the employer will rectify the problems. Too often they continue to work in horrific conditions because their family needs the income.

Even when employees break down because of a Red

Work Zone and have to take time off to recover, they often have to do battle with the employer or the insurance company to receive the benefits to which they are entitled. Because the system is far more powerful than the individual, it can withhold payments and demand multiple proofs of illness, which is exhausting and demoralizing for those already depressed and depleted from their struggle within the work environment. Thus, recovery from the Red Work Zone becomes further complicated by the Red Work System. To recover from the Red Work Zone, supportive relatives, friends and therapists play a valuable role.

Harry continued to progress in therapy, which led him to write again.

Dear Dr. Sohail

It has now been little more than a year since I first met you and sought your counsel. To say that much has happened or changed in my life since that fateful encounter, would be an extreme understatement. And although it sometimes seems hard to believe, I have with your help, succeeded in obtaining a new lease on life. For that, I can not thank you enough.

When I first met you I was totally exhausted and by all accounts dysfunctional. I was living in the darkest spectrum of the red zone, miserable and barely existing. You quickly ascertained that my poisoned and stressful work environment was detrimental to my health, and was the underlying cause of my failed family relationship. Leaving that work environment was one of the hardest decisions I've ever had to make. I felt diminished and weak, and thought of myself as a complete failure. Eventually, however, I began to understand the significance and necessity of that decision, and how it facilitated my recovery, and relationship with my family.

The second significant change occurred a few months later, after your meetings with my wife and daughters. Though my relationship with them was becoming somewhat more normal, it really began to change for the better after their meetings with you. Our communication became more frequent, meaningful, relaxed and spontaneous.

During the summer months I went camping and canoeing with all of them, individually, which gave us all a chance to reconnect with one another. We began to relax, laugh, and see each other in a totally new light. Since then, my relationship with my family has flourished. In September our daughters returned to their respective towns to continue their University studies. I talk to them on the phone at least once every week, often at length. We often meet for lunch or dinner, go grocery shopping, or take in a show. We are, I believe, functioning and getting along as never before, and truly enjoying each other's company. These wonderful experiences have made me realize how much we care for each other and how much I missed their presence and affection over the last several years. I am enormously grateful and happy to once again be a part of their lives.

I have without a doubt been living in the Green Zone for the last nine months. It feels absolutely wonderful. At times though, it scares me a little, for it all seems so surreal, like a dream. I have lived in the Red Zone for such a long time, that I have lost the sense of what it's like to be living in peace and happiness. I am however very determined not to return there again.

On a less positive note; I have not returned to work yet. I have made several attempts to do so, but each time I go back to my old job, I seem to plunge into the Red Zone and experience severe anxiety and physical discomfort. I am it seems, unable to reconcile with the negative experiences of that part of my life. And although this causes me considerable anguish, I am determined not to let it dominate my newfound life. I keep busy with volunteer work, and often undertake other types of work projects. In the near future I will be eligible for retirement from teaching, and look forward to the day when I can leave the world of education behind, and move on to the Green Zone work projects.

Once again thank you for all you did for me and my family. I feel extremely fortunate to have met you when I was down and out. Your insight, philosophy and wisdom have been most thought provoking and have prompted me to closely examine my life and my actions, and to re-evaluate my priorities. Slowly, I am learning to look at my relationships in a different, less serious and constrained, and more tolerant, accepting, and positive way.

Thank you for changing my life.

Harry

SOCIAL/COMMUNITY ZONES

After people recognize the dynamics of their Family and Work Systems, I encourage them to focus on their relationship with their community, which includes the neighbourhood, as well as all social, religious or political organizations in which they are involved.

Green Zone Communities are based on democratic and secular humanistic principles. People are treated equally irrespective of their religious, political, linguistic and ethnic affiliations. On the other hand, Yellow and Red Zone Communities are capable of fostering attitudes of ignorance, poverty and prejudice. It is not easy to live in the Green Zone emotionally if one is part of a Red Zone Community. Even in those countries which apparently score high in surveys of their commitment to Human Rights, there can be certain communities that are very prejudiced and treat minorities unjustly and unfairly.

One description of a Red Zone Community was narrated to me by University Professor Najam, who emigrated to England for a few years. He later moved to Canada where he is now living happily in a Green Zone Community.

My Dear Dr. Sohail

You have asked me to share with you how I felt when my family and I were the targets and victims of racial attacks from a few bad neighbours in England. As you know, hatred and discrimination hurt, and hurt more the people who are sensitive and do not wish to think ill of others and who are not used to using words like "inferior" and "superior" to classify people.

I arrived at Preston, Scotland in September 1995 to continue my studies from the University of Punjab (Lahore, Pakistan) where I worked as an assistant professor for many years. Unfortunately, very shortly after my arrival in UK, a range of unpleasant incidents and events began to affect my perception of the civilized world and the people of the developed nations. I wish to demonstrate the cumulative effect of difficulties created by the bad neighbours during the period that I spent in Preston.

There is a long-standing history of racial abuse, harassment and assault on me, which have never been satisfactorily understood and resolved. One of the most disruptive experiences has been the need to change addresses repeatedly due to racial harassment. This included the throwing of bottles, bricks and stones both at us and at the house. My children and I were stopped and kicked or punched in the street and in the playground. Physical threats, verbal abuse and obscenities became a commonplace occurrence. More specific details about the most severe episodes are cited below of the difficulties experienced in the months prior to my departure for Canada.

The changes of addresses were as follows:

St. George's Road. I left after two weeks due to threats and intimidation.

Fishwick Parade. I left after seven months following persistent harassment. Police was informed but offered little assistance.

New Townley Road. My son was persistently molested, bullied and intimidated.

Surrey Street. I remained there until harassment and assaults on myself, my family and property became intolerable and I had to leave the city and the country.

In December 1995, several glass bottles were thrown at the door of my house. This vandalism continued for some time. I did not find police helpful and became very disillusioned about my future. On at least four occasions physical threats were made and we had to put up with comments like, "Paki leave the area or else face the consequences."

The police were informed when our family and friends visiting from the Netherlands had to leave prematurely because their car was seriously damaged, twice. They left feeling very distressed.

In August 1997, my only surviving son contracted Meningitis (I had already lost my other precious son in Pakistan only a few years earlier). My son's illness caused my family and me a great deal of anxiety and interfered with my studies. The accumulation of grief and fear made my wife clinically depressed. She also developed an ulcer and required surgery. This caused immense disruption in my household and I had to take sole charge of three young children while my wife was hospitalized during her convalescence.

My son who was very young suffered a great deal as he was exposed to the immense negativity and extremely damaging words. The racial comments made him depressed and he started to blame himself. The racially motivated hate-saturated remarks influenced his innocent trail of thoughts. He was constantly reminded of his cultural heritage in a negative way. Words like "Ugly face Paki" became part of his daily routine.

He saw a counsellor who left him worse than before. He received lectures, not therapy, explanations, not consolation. I believe a warm hug and a few minutes of patient listening mends more hearts than the most learned lectures. So the bad environment proved detrimental to the health of my son and my family.

Finally we left England and came to Canada, as I believe, "Although the world is full of suffering, it is also full of the overcoming of it."

Najam

It is not uncommon for people who live in Red Social/ Community Zones to finally leave that community, or even country, to travel to a Green Zone Community where they can live in peace and harmony with their neighbours. Many refugees from countries all over the world belong to that group.

Part Four

JOURNEY FROM THE RED ZONE TO THE GREEN ZONE

NIGHTMARES

A psychoanalyst and colleague of mine, who had been seeing Ryan twice a week, referred him to me. Ryan had been suffering from terrible nightmares for years. Therapy had helped him understand the symbolic meanings of his symptoms and family dynamics, but failed to stop the unwanted visits of his nightmares.

After his assessment I offered him a combination of individual, marital, family and group therapy and introduced him to the Green, Yellow, and Red Zone concept. In the beginning he was very analytical, but gradually I shared with him that the goal of therapy *is to change and not just to understand*. Understanding was a bonus. I wanted to help him connect with his present and leave the past behind. Whenever he was in a crisis or faced a stressful situation, he automatically regressed to when he was eight, that sad time when his mother had abandoned him. I encouraged him to face his life situations as an adult, connect and disconnect with his family, friends and students and do it in the here and now.

Once Ryan accepted my philosophy, his progress began. Within a few months he started spending a continually increasing amount of time in the Green Zone.

Gradually he started sleeping better and needed to see me less often. His clinical visits have been reduced to once a month for follow-up sessions. He is so thrilled that he can enjoy a peaceful sleep. His wife is pleased to have her husband back and functioning like a proper partner.

When I had seen Ryan's wife initially she was very pessimistic as the problem was longstanding and very disruptive to their marriage and family life. I saw her a few times to offer her support and encourage her to become more optimistic. When Ryan got better, I acknowledged the hard work she had done by staying with him and supporting her husband through the difficult periods of regression and family upheaval.

It is rewarding for Ryan's family and fellow group members to see the positive results of hard work. In one of Ryan's sessions I interviewed him for my book. He felt proud to share his story, hoping that it would help others.

Sohail: I would like to focus on the Green, Yellow, and Red Zone Model and explore how it affected your therapy and progress. Can you share with me how this concept helped you in understanding and dealing with your emotional problems?

Ryan: I found the concept very helpful especially because I am a visual person. I could easily visualize the colours. I could feel that when I was in the Red Zone I was in the ditch and I was on the highway when I was in the Green. In the beginning of the therapy, becoming aware of how I was doing, from day to day, was very important and this concept was helpful. After becoming aware of my own Zones, I also became aware of other people's Zones before I interacted with them and that helped me in my relationships. The next step was to recognize when I was going into the Red Zone and find ways to prevent it and then find ways to get out of the Red Zone even if I fell into it, into the ditch.

S: Can you provide me with an example?

R: I found it helpful with my kids. I often lost my temper in the past, but now I can catch myself before that happens. I can stop before any damage is done. This morning while I was playing with my children, one of them knocked my glasses. I was so upset I was going to push him, but then I immediately realized I was going into the Red Zone so I stopped. I was still angry but I did not lay a hand on him. Since I learned this concept I am using humor to stay in the Green Zone. Last week in my class I saw a girl reading a love letter rather than paying attention to the lecture. I looked at her, smiled and said, "If I collected all my love letters from high school, it would make an encyclopedia." She smiled and put it away. So I was able to get my message across and still stay in the Green Zone.

S: When you came here for therapy, were you living in the Red Zone?

R: Looking back now, I think I have lived in the Red Zone off and on since my childhood. It got worse when I started having nightmares for the last ten years, which you referred to my over 3000 consecutive nights of nightmares. It started when a troubled adolescent girl falsely accused me of sexual assault. It was a terrifying experience. After that incident, parents stopped sending their children to our house to play. That was quite humiliating. After I was exonerated and proved innocent, she made another accusation three weeks later, and the police had to investigate the case. That terrifying experience dug up the unconscious fear lying dormant in my mind since my childhood.

S: What happened when you were a child?

R: When I was eight, my mother suffered from depression. She became abusive and was finally hospitalized for two years. For those two years I felt abandoned.

S: You mentioned to me that, as an adult, you discussed your past with your mother.

R: Yes, I met with my mom and I cried and I asked her, "Why did you not love me as a child? Was there anything wrong with me?" Listening to my concerns my mother apologized and asked for my forgiveness. After that exchange she went into another episode of depression for which she was hospitalized and received good care, unlike 1958 when medicine was not as advanced. People used to be locked up in mental hospitals.

S: You also mentioned that she has a good relationship with your children.

R: Yes, she is a wonderful grandmother. She loves our two children. In January she phoned us and said, "I am 81 and I am not going to be around forever. I want to see my grandchildren. Send them over for March break." We said we could not afford the airfare. She sent them tickets and they had a really nice time.

S: So after you were wrongfully accused at school by a teenager, you started having nightmares and night terrors. Tell me more about them.

R: I suffered. I really suffered. It started right after the incident in which I was accused and I could never put the genie back in the bottle. After the police investigation started I could never have a peaceful sleep. I had four years of therapy with a psychoanalyst. He helped me a lot but the nightmares did not get better. I just learned to cope with them.

S: What was a typical night for you?

R: I would go to bed and fall asleep immediately but then wake up sweating as early as 1:00 a.m. I used to have constant terrifying nightmares in which I was being attacked by bears. My therapist believed bears represented my anger. He said I had tremendous anger that I was unable to express.

S: Who were you angry with?

R: I was angry with my mother who had abandoned me for two years when I was eight.

S: How often did you see your analyst?

R: Twice a week for four years. I used to keep a voice-activated tape recorder. In the middle of the night I used to dictate my nightmare in the tape recorder in great detail and then in my sessions I used to play the tape and my analyst analyzed it for me. I used to feel like a little boy who was terrified.

S: What happened that you were referred to our clinic?

R: I think my analyst believed he had taken me as far as he could. There was a year's waiting list for your clinic, so I spent one more year separating from my analyst. There was a strong transference so separating was not easy, in fact it was extremely painful. I had even taken over one of the children's teddy bears. I used to hug it when I went to bed.

S: So how did you feel when you came to see me?

R: I did not want to be here. I didn't think I was mentally ill. I thought I just needed to get the demons out of me so I wasn't terrorized with nightmares. Since I felt betrayed by my mother, I did not feel close to people. I did not trust people. So when you invited me for group therapy I did not want to come. I did not want to connect with people. I did not want to share my story with others.

S: Now after two years of therapy, how do you feel you were able to progress from the Red Zone to the Green Zone?

R: I experienced an emotional change in the last two years. I realized I needed to connect with people. I realized I needed to be close to my wife and children, my loved ones that I had pushed away. It started with my caring for the group members. It was a gradual process. I came to group regularly and religiously. Nothing prevented me from coming. I was committed to the process and I think it played an important role in my getting better. I was absolutely determined to become better because my life was hell.

S: How do you think individual sessions complemented the group sessions?

R: Things happened in the group that I processed in individual sessions. When one of the group members said, "I am an abuser," I did not think twice about it in the group but that woke me up at 1:00 a.m. with night sweats. So I needed to come for an individual session to process that. I realized how other people's comments affected me. I became aware of my Zones and how I could slide into the Red Zone without knowing where I was going. Once I saw the movie, The Red Violin, I enjoyed it with my wife but then had a terrifying nightmare about it. As I started to recognize what was going on, I had more control to stay in my Green Zone.

S: What Zone do you live in now?

R: Now I have been living in my Green Zone most of the time. Even if I fall into the Red Zone I understand where I am and quickly recover.

S: What does it feel like to live in the Green Zone?

R: I can sleep comfortably. I have been sleeping well for the last four months. After having insomnia for years it is a great blessing. I cannot believe I lasted that long without proper sleep. Now I look forward to being involved with different things. I enjoy meeting people and socializing. I feel happier and healthier than before. I feel stronger and more confident. I like myself and feel more optimistic. My relationship with my wife and children has improved. I was afraid I was going to lose them. Living in the Green Zone is wonderful. I feel better now than I ever felt in my whole life. I think I lived in the Red Zone for most of my life. I think this is the first time that I have been living regularly in the Green Zone. It is just wonderful. I cannot believe I am so well.

S: Any suggestions for others who live in the Red Zone?

R: I think people should recognize when they are living in the Red Zone. That is a lot of work needed once they recognize that dilemma. Many people develop physical symptoms. When they are suffering from ulcers or colitis they believe it is all physical. I could not blame it on physical health so I had to face the fact that my problem was emotional.

S: You worked very hard in therapy. I was quite impressed by your dedication and commitment.

R: Yes, it was a lot of hard work but it was worth it.

S: Thank you very much for sharing your story. I am confident it will help others. Your story will inspire them and give them hope. They need to be able to realize that they can change their lives with proper professional help. They can take that first step on the journey that will help with their progress from the Red Zone to the Green Zone where they can lead a happy and healthy life.

Thanks once again, Ryan.

MILESTONES OF A THERAPEUTIC JOURNEY FROM THE RED ZONE TO THE GREEN ZONE

I met Catherine in November 1999. During my assessment it became quite apparent that she had been living in the Red Zone for many years. She was very frustrated, unhappy and depressed. She appeared to be struggling with many unresolved issues:

- She hated her job in the bank and found it so stressful that she finally quit.
- She was grieving her parents' deaths.
- She had a personality that was full of anger and resentment. She had become very judgmental of others. Over the years she had alienated her friends, relatives and colleagues.
- She had ongoing conflicts with her children. Her daughter had run away from home at the age of 16 and her son did not know how to cope with his mother. Unfortunately Catherine had no insight into her personality and blamed others for her unhappiness. There was no awareness of how badly she affected others. She was lucky to have a husband who was a kind, generous

person, and a friend, Monique, who was very supportive and understanding.

After my initial assessment I offered Catherine a combination of individual, family and group therapy. She readily agreed. I suggested that if she worked hard with me I could gradually help her to lead a healthy and happy life. I asked her to keep a journal and faithfully record her feelings and the significant events of her day-to-day life. I was pleased to see that in spite of her emotional difficulties, she was very open, honest and straightforward when discussing her problems. Because she had had to wait for a long time to get into the clinic to see me, she had become very motivated and was quite willing to follow my recommendations.

After a few sessions, I introduced her to my concept of the Green, Yellow and Red Zones. She tried very hard to understand the concept and apply it during her therapy and day-to-day life.

Catherine worked on her journal regularly and she brought it for me to read during each therapy session. As she became more comfortable, we gradually focused on the nature of her interactions with others, which kept her and all her relationships in the Red Zone.

As she became more interested in writing about her life, I asked her to describe her experiences growing up with her family. One day she brought the following detailed account of her family background, which was quite helpful in understanding the evolution of her idealistic and perfectionist personality, and judgmental lifestyle.

Dr. Sohail

I was born in 1952 and grew up in a fairly small town where the population was about 8,000. I was part of a middle-class family with parents who stayed married until death parted them. I can remember watching "Leave it to Beaver," "Lassie," and "Jonathan Griffith," and thought that I lived in a pretty average home. I was a middle child in an unusual way. I had twin sisters nine years older, and a brother nine years younger.

My mother was a stay-at-home mom until I was twelve. When I was born my father had wanted a boy so badly that they didn't even have a name chosen for a girl. So when they came up with my name it was the closest female version my dad could come up with that was similar to his first two names. My mother had lost a baby in between the birth of my sisters and me. I have often wondered how different I may have turned out had that child lived. However, I wasn't about to let my dad down. So I was determined to be the best darned person next to a son that he ever could have had. As I grew up I shadowed him. We went fishing together, skating together. He took me to ride a pony one of his friends from work owned. We went there quite often. I always tried to do my absolute best at school because I wanted them to be very proud of me.

By the time I was six my sisters were fifteen. When I wanted to follow them around they always told Mom and Dad I was pestering them and getting into their stuff in their room. I definitely felt like an outsider. They were in their teens and interested in boys. That started a whole new set of problems. My father was a very possessive person. Actually, as I look back now, he was exactly like his mother. She was a very strong woman who had seven sons and every one toed the line around her right up until she died. My father never married until he was thirty-two and grandma never approved of my mother. My mother was Anglican prior to taking instruction in the Catholic faith — so she could marry my dad. Grandma could not have approved otherwise.

When my sisters wanted to date and see their friends outside of school, all hell broke loose. Dad didn't want them to go out with boys, go out to a restaurant or anywhere else. They began to do those things behind his back. When he found out, the fighting and arguing was unbearable. My mom didn't seem to object as much because I think she felt all of that was a normal part of growing up but what Dad said was what mattered. One time my sister started seeing a guy and my dad found out and said she should introduce him to her parents. So she brought him over. In conversation Dad asked him what religion he was. When the chap answered he was an Atheist my dad threw him out of the house. This continued on until the twins were in Grade 12. One night they came home late and my dad literally spanked them all the way upstairs (we had a two-storey house). There was a huge fight again, and the twins packed their bags and moved to Toronto.

There wasn't any more fighting about boys but it created a huge rift in our family. My mom didn't want them to move out but what could she do? I thought things were looking up because I got their bedroom, which was a lot bigger than my old one.

Shortly after my eighth birthday, my mother

became pregnant. Back then things were very hush-hush. Not like now, when there is nothing left to the imagination. I had thought everyone was quite happy with me but I guess I was fooling myself. My dad had never given up the idea of having a son. A real son, not just some girl who was trying her darndest to fit the mould. By the time my brother was born my mom was forty and my dad fifty-three.

I couldn't go to the hospital but my mom sent a little letter home to me with my dad every day when he went to see her in the hospital. She tried her best to make me feel a part of what was happening. Once they brought my baby brother home I knew nothing would ever be the same again. I knew my dad still loved me but now there was this son that I would always have to live up to. I would have to perfect my ways of doing things so I'd always remain in my dad's favour.

As I grew into adolescence I began to have a growing interest in boys. I wanted to play sports after school but my mom worked on an afternoon shift and expected me to stay home and look after my brother. I was also expected to cook supper and do the dishes. I did my homework once I had finished all that. Though I suppose deep down I resented having to do all this, I never really questioned it. I just figured it was the right thing to do because it was expected of me — so I did it.

When I was thirteen, we moved from the house that my parents had built. We moved all the way across town to where I knew nobody. The next year I started high school. Increasingly I was interested in boys. One day the son of the people who had bought our old house, walked me home from school. My mother told me before she left for work, "Your dad has seen you two together and he told me to tell you that you better tell the boy not to walk you home. If you don't tell him, your father said he will."

I could tell this wasn't my mother's doing, but I knew from what had happened with my sisters years before, I had better be ready to leave home or comply. I hadn't the spunk to leave so I told him. No other boy ever walked me home from school again. Ever.

As a teenager I had a very good relationship with my mom. We could talk about anything. She took me shopping. She never drove a car so we got a cab uptown or took the bus to the mall. We used to have lunch together and she ordered me milkshakes. To this day when I have a milkshake I think of her.

I only went out on two or three dates with boys from my class when I was in Grade 12. My dad drove us to the show and came and picked us up. I didn't pursue any further dates. I could sense my dad wasn't pleased — he would have this funny way of pursing his lips and I could tell he was ticked off. The man I eventually married was the nephew of a couple that Mom and Dad had known since I was born. She worked with my mom. One night they came over to play cards with Mom and Dad and they brought their nephew with them. That was May 9, 1970. He asked me to marry him the first of August. Then he came over and asked my parents. My mom almost had a stroke because I was only seventeen. But my dad liked him, and he consented — then I almost had a stroke. We were married on the first day of May 1971.

Since Catherine kept her diary current and brought it each time she attended her session, she agreed that I could quote excerpts from it and share my impressions that would help to highlight the milestones of her fourteen-month therapeutic journey from the Red Zone to the Green Zone. She covered that long distance in a very short time.

> *Sunday November 21*
> *I agreed to keep my grandson Evan overnight with me so that my son Brent and his partner Colleen could enjoy their party. I put him to bed early because he was fussy and I thought he would never stop crying. I thought I would tear my hair out. He finally fell asleep only to wake at 11 p.m. He woke up every hour until 4 a.m. and then slept for two more hours until 6 a.m. Needless to say I didn't get any sleep. When I took Evan home at 11:30 Sunday morning, I saw that there were three friends who stayed overnight. Colleen and one of the fellows had not even been to bed. Brent went to sleep about 4:30 a.m. and was just getting up. "How bloody immature this scene looks." I don't think they went out. I think they stayed home and I got to look after their son. The more I thought of it the more angry I became. I felt used and taken advantage of.*

Catherine was so guided by a sense of responsibility in her life that she had no concept of fun. She perceived all recreational activities as a waste of time and the reflection of an irresponsible lifestyle. She was very critical of her son. Rather than enjoying her time with her grandson, she resented him because she felt that her son was manipulating her.

She was not only judgmental of her son, she was also critical of her sister-in-law who had fun playing with her children.

> *Wednesday November 24*
> *My sister-in-law Pam and I went shopping today. We had preplanned the day about two and a half weeks before because she always has to be home to take her children to and from school. I don't think she wanted to go all day but she did. She coddles her kids to the point where I find it unbearable.*

When I tried to understand the dynamics and evolution of her anger, I became aware of the sadness and depression she felt when her parents died. She had unresolved grief that came to the surface at special times in the year, especially Christmas.

> *Wednesday, November 24*
> *I hate Christmas. Ever since Mom died I don't care if it ever comes. Since I lost my father I really don't care. I just seem to go through all the motions because it's expected. But again, I feel like I am someone else looking in at everyone else having a good time. Inside, though my heart feels broken like everything else, I can't seem to fix it.*

Since Catherine could not enjoy life herself, it was very difficult for her to see others enjoying themselves and having fun. She seemed to be jealous of the happiness of other people.

Catherine's biggest and most painful conflict was with

her daughter, Laura, who had run away from home at 16, as she could not cope with her mother's judgmental attitude. Catherine had not seen her for seven years, then she encountered her by chance. They reconciled briefly, and Catherine had a baby shower for her. The day after that shower, Laura mysteriously disappeared once again. Catherine felt betrayed. Shortly after Catherine started therapy she unexpectedly ran into Laura again in the doctor's office.

Thursday November 25
I did not bother to tell Robert I had run into Laura in the clinic. I have not seen her since April 11, the day I held a baby shower for her. I turned around and ran smack into her in the waiting room so she couldn't avoid me there. She acted like I had just seen her a few days before. She said, "I want you to meet Ken." I then said, "Who is that, a NEW MAN in your life?" I actually should have said the NEWEST because she goes through men like I go through socks. They were on their way to Oshawa and she said they would stop by on their way home if time permitted. They did, for 40 minutes, and we traded polite talk. I felt like I was sitting with a stranger. I was thinking to myself, "I feel like I have absolutely no connection with you." I don't believe a word that comes out of her mouth anyway. She has lied to us so much since leaving home nearly seven years ago that I almost find it unbearable to even talk to her at times. Robert says I should not place so much importance on that but I feel that if she isn't being truthful with me then what is there left in the relationship? Anyway, they left shortly and I was glad. After only 40

minutes I had had more than enough.

Catherine was especially judgmental about Laura's romantic life. Catherine did not approve of her daughter's dating, a replay of the way her father had disapproved of hers. Catherine had very high moral and ethical standards. Those standards were so unrealistic that her daughter felt suffocated by her expectations. Robert, on the other hand was very nurturing, supportive and forgiving. He encouraged Catherine to relax and let others enjoy life but she could not. Catherine believed that sex belonged only inside the institution of marriage. She could not accept that if two people loved each other they could have a loving and intimate relationship without the blessings of the church. In her eyes it was a sin.

Thursday November 25
Then I thought back to when Brent used to bring his girlfriend over to our house and they slept together downstairs — against our wishes. I was very angry. They had no regard for my feelings at all. Perhaps if they had they wouldn't have ended up with a baby born out of wedlock. But hey, it's 1999, and I'm supposed to mind my own business. Marriage isn't cool anymore. It's a good job Laura didn't get married. She would have had to hire a private lawyer just to handle her divorces at the rate she changes partners.

Catherine always expressed her feelings very bluntly and did not hesitate to use cutting comments and sarcastic remarks. She believed she was being honest but some of those comments were very cruel.

When I inquired about their past relationship, I discovered that after Laura left home, she was dating a man that Catherine disapproved of. To avoid her mother's harsh attitude, Laura severed all ties with her family. After a while someone told Catherine that Laura had to appear in court as her boyfriend was in some legal trouble. Catherine went uninvited to court and gave Laura the following letter.

Laura,

We don't know where to start or what to say to you that could make us understand why you are doing this. Did you need that much freedom from us that you chose to live with a person like Ross just to spite us? The sad thing is though now you have no freedom. You have allowed this man (and we use the term loosely) to control and to manipulate your every thought and move so that you have no contact with any of your family at all. Do you hate us all that much or is Ross that insecure that he can't let you have a life other than with him? You now have an infant to care for. She isn't some pet you can pretend isn't hungry down at the barn and ignore while you have a few extra hours sleep. You are now about to embark on 20 years of hard work and if your daughter takes it upon herself to treat you, like you have treated your dad and me over the last 16 months, you will soon see it's a pretty thankless job. For months we have wondered and blamed ourselves but with the help of others around us, we aren't blaming ourselves anymore. Last summer we spent weekend after weekend trying to find you. I phoned Nan and told her about your school friend, who was killed. Dad phoned a number of times, including twice on Friday night. Did she give you all those messages? If you want to contact us you know our phone number. You also know we're not home until after 4:00 p.m. Don't try to "pull my chain" anymore by calling me at work, because I won't take your calls there anymore. All the people there know what's going on with you so it's no surprise to them. Ross is a big talker and has a big mouth when it comes to standing over your shoulder, controlling everything you say or do. But why wouldn't you call your dad and talk to him? Maybe once Ross goes away and says "Bye, Bye," you will. Maybe with God's help you will get your backbone back. One can only feel sorry for a daughter who is doing what you are doing. Do you even stop to think what you have given up? The completion of your high school education; a promising future in the RCMP if you had stayed with it; a job at the mushroom farm, which was not fantastic but at least it was honest money; and last but not least, your adolescence. You have let him rob you of all this. Why are you running from your family? Are you ashamed of your own actions or of him? We went to court Wednesday to show you we supported you. He has a long history of abusing not only the system but women and children as well. We thought maybe you felt helpless and had no one to turn to. It could be just a matter of time before you become the next girlfriend who took a rap for some crime he commits. Hopefully, you will wake up before it's too late. Unless you have given up your faith for him too, you should remember the story of the Prodigal son. The moral of the story was that no matter how much the one son had done wrong his father still loved him unconditionally and welcomed him home. No matter how much you have hurt us, that is how we love you.

Mom

After receiving the letter, Laura was very upset. In a few weeks she sent the following letter expressing her feelings and asking them to stay out of her life. She had had enough of them.

Mom and Dad

I would like to start off by letting you know that this letter is written in my own words. I'm telling you this because you seem to think that Ross controls everything that I say or do. Well you are wrong! I am my own person, as is Ross. If I choose to do something I'll do it whether or not someone tells me not to, and you should know that better than anyone. You asked me in your letter if I'm with "a person like Ross" just to spite you? Well, now I'm going to ask you a question, "How do you know what kind of a person Ross is? You never ever gave him a fair chance, and if you had given him half a chance you would have found out that he is a kind, loving, hard working, fun person to be with. Ross is the kind of person that once he's your friend, he is your friend for life. He would go out of his way to help you in any way he could. But you don't see these qualities in him like I do, because you were set against him from the very beginning.

To me Ross is a man (and I use that word strongly).

He is not insecure nor does he try to control or manipulate me. I chose not to contact you on my own free will. If you owe Ross anything it's a little gratitude because if it wasn't for him I wouldn't have contacted you as soon as I did.

Yes we do have an infant and if you care to know your granddaughter's name it is Rose. She was born on August 10, 1995 and weighed 5lb. 10oz. I would have called and told you but I wasn't interested in hearing your voice and your opinion on how you think Ross has so-called 'robbed me of my adolescence.' Ross hasn't robbed me of anything; in fact he has given me his love and companionship. He has been there when I needed a shoulder to cry on and to talk to. He has listened to me ramble on about nothing at all but most of all he has given me his friendship.

You say that having children is a pretty thankless job, well if that is what you feel, then fine. Thanks for worrying, thanks for trying to find me. Thank you for anything you have ever done for me my whole life. Oh yeah, and thanks for going to court and butting your noses in where they did not belong. That is a real good way of showing me you love me. You say Ross has a big mouth, but he does not! You do when it comes to voicing your opinion where it isn't needed or wanted. Do me a favour and don't feel sorry for a daughter like me because I am a big girl and I can take care of myself. You told me if I ever need your help I know how to get hold of you, but if your kind of help is like what you tried to do in court, I don't ever want it.

I am not ashamed of my actions and I am certainly not ashamed of Ross. I am very proud of him. I am however ashamed of you and your actions, because I thought you guys were more open-minded when it came to giving someone a chance. Is that not what you taught me? To give people a chance and to always keep an open mind? Maybe you should practise what you preach.

How do you know what Ross's history is like? Have you known him since he has a child? No! You haven't, so stop bad-mouthing someone you don't even know. I am not helpless and I don't have to wake up because I am already wide awake. You guys are the ones who need to wake up and realize that I have my own life which includes Ross and our daughter, Rose, and if you don't like it then that's just too bad.

I love Ross and he loves me and no matter how long he is in jail, I will wait for him. And if you can't accept our relationship then I don't want you involved in my life ever.

Laura

While Catherine struggled with her relationship with her children and relatives, she was lucky to have a good relationship with her husband Robert who was a hard working man. He lived in the Green Zone and ignored the feelings within Catherine that came from her Red Zone. I was quite impressed by his honesty, sincerity and integrity. He loved Catherine and believed she was a good woman at heart. He saw her as an orange — tough, bitter peel but sweet inside. She acknowledged his positive influence on her.

Wednesday December 1
Robert and I have spent the last three days doing some odd jobs around the house and we also went shopping. I enjoy doing stuff with him because we don't normally have time like this to spend together. I can be myself with him. I don't have to walk around issues with him. If I have something to say I just say it.

Catherine was also lucky to have a good friend Monique, who like Robert, lived in the Green Zone and cared a lot for Catherine. The women once worked together and, although Catherine was on sick leave, they still met together for coffee once a week. Those meetings were a highlight for Catherine.

Wednesday December 8
At lunch today I had coffee with Monique, someone I have known for twelve years. I worked with her at Bowmanville. Her and I and Donna (who is about 60 years old) still keep in touch. Donna retired in October of this year. She just could not take any more of what the bank is doing to people. I know how she feels. The thought of going back to work makes me sick. I don't think I can think of one positive thing about the place right now. Monique is French Canadian and she reads the book THE PROPHET. *She is good to talk to. She is a good listener. She has two boys, 15 and 18 years old, and she has a unique relationship with them. I envy her at times. We are trying to have coffee once a week just to chat. I look forward to spending an hour with her.*

In many ways Monique was a role model for Catherine. She not only looked up to Monique, she also envied her affectionate relationship with her children. Monique was a constant source of support and inspiration for Catherine and I encouraged her to continue to develop that relationship.

Alongside morality issues, Catherine was also very sensitive about finances. She believed that Laura was not only sexually irresponsible but also financially incompetent. She did not sympathize with her economic struggles. Rather than supporting she was always critical and judgmental.

Thursday December 9
I can't believe the nerve Laura has. After eight months of not so much as "Hello" she wants us to back a car loan. The only question I did ask her was why didn't Ken get the loan. She said he can't because he is in the process of a bankruptcy and they won't let him borrow. Boy he sure sounds like a winner to me now. God Almighty, where does she get these men from anyway? It won't surprise me if we never hear from her again now — and if you want my opinion right now — I could care less!

Catherine had an ongoing conflict with Brent and Colleen about baby-sitting Evan. On one hand she could not be assertive enough to say "No" to them, and on the other hand she could not enjoy looking after her grandson. She was forever full of resentment.

Monday December 13
Colleen asked on the phone, "Oh, I was wondering if you would like to keep Evan overnight Saturday again. It is my office Christmas party Saturday. If you don't want to I suppose we can ask someone else." This time I thought for a couple of seconds and said, "Well, I have to check with Dad first to see if we have any plans." Robert was gone to a union meeting. I then told her if we were not doing anything else I would baby-sit, but did not commit to it. If every time I talk to them I am going to get hit with another baby-sitting request, I am going to start to avoid talking to them. I am beginning to feel that is all they associate me with.

I asked Catherine to invite Brent to the next session. During our meeting Catherine felt quite relieved when Brent told her that she did not have to baby-sit Evan if she did not want to. All she had to say was "No" and they would have made alternative arrangements. Then I requested a meeting with Robert and Catherine.

Friday December 17
Robert and I went to see Dr. Sohail today. I knew it would seem strange to Robert because he definitely doesn't view things like me and I don't think men like to talk about their feelings as women do. He brought out some good points though.

I discussed with Robert my plans for working with Catherine, which involved helping her to be more accepting of people and relaxing some of her perfectionist attitudes towards herself and others. He agreed with my assessment and was supportive of the direction that therapy was taking.

Besides being angry with family members, Catherine was also very bruised by her bank's attitude. She believed they did not care about their customers. The work environment had become so toxic that she could not survive there anymore. Her work environment had turned into a Red Zone.

> *Saturday December 18*
> *The bank right now is only interested in people for the way they can make more money. They don't give a damn about you as a person. They throw people around like dogs and internally, as an organization, coldly disregard how their staff feels about what they do to them. However they put on this big corporate front to the public saying they value their people. If the public only knew what a crock that was.*

On special occasions Catherine remembered her parents and felt depressed.

> *Monday December 20*
> *Today would have been Dad's 89th birthday. God how I miss him. I think back to when he was well and how he used to love to come over and visit Robert and me and the kids. I cry just thinking about him and my mom. I miss them both so much I can't even begin to tell anyone how much. I know my children won't miss me like that when I die. That is probably a good thing though. Then their hearts won't keep breaking over and over like mine does.*

Since Robert was more nurturing and accepting of Laura and her boyfriend Ken, I encouraged Catherine to spend some time with them at Christmas. I was hoping that gradually she could abandon her judgmental attitude and develop a loving relationship with her daughter. Christmas seemed a good time to initiate such interaction. I was also encouraging Catherine to become aware of her Zones and try her best in social situations not to leave her Green Zone.

> *Monday December 27*
> *After supper Robert and Laura's boyfriend Ken went downstairs to play darts. The two of them seemed to hit if off well together. But then Robert gets along with everyone. It's me that's the Wicked Witch of the West. Laura and I chatted about safe generic topics. I wanted to make sure to steer clear of any conversation that would take me out of my Green Zone. I managed it too. We left about 9:00 p.m. all agreeing not to be strangers in the future. It remains to be seen how the relationship will proceed from here.*

Whenever Catherine worked hard to stay in the Green Zone, I acknowledged her attempts. It seemed that she valued my nurturing comments. I gradually realized that her father was also very critical of her when she was growing up. She never felt fully accepted. She believed he wanted a son. So my accepting and encouraging her helped her accept herself and make progress in therapy.

One of the painful areas in her life was her job. She had been so hurt emotionally that she could not imagine going back to work, and since that was the only work she had done all her life, she could not think of doing anything else.

Friday January 7
I absolutely hate going to Toronto to work. I never have liked it, but when they took away my job twice in less than one year, I had little choice. I have kept telling myself (and everyone else) that it was okay, but eventually the fears came out. I feel like I am suffocating when I think about it.

Catherine really got upset whenever she received a letter or phone calls from work. Such interactions put her in the Red Zone. I had to help her to not answer the telephone and instead bring the letters to me to read and then we would decide how to respond.

Friday January 14
I felt a lot better after seeing Dr. Sohail today. I think he was glad to see that I had shown self-control talking on the phone to my supervisor who was very rude and disrespectful. What he said was true, because I guess I am hoping I will get some empathy and comfort from these people but it is not likely to happen. They do not care how I feel, they only care about the bank and the stupid cold function I perform for them.

We talked about my love for animals. They never judge you. They like you just for being you, and for wanting to be with them. He suggested that I talk to his nurse Anne about volunteering at the Humane Society. So I did. I think it will do me a lot of good because I really miss having animals around.

As I explored her anger towards work, I also pursued her alternate interests. It seemed as though she liked animals and farm life. I encouraged her to do volunteer work with animals. I thought it ironic that the woman who judged everyone so harshly, even her children, liked animals because she believed they did not judge.

As therapy progressed, it became evident that being judged by her father and living in the Red Zone for a number of years had had a major impact on her self-esteem. She felt like a failure as a mother as well as a worker. It was nice to see how her husband reassured and consoled her, as she felt down and judged herself as critically as she judged others.

> *Friday January 28*
> *As we were lying there, I started to cry. Robert asked me what was wrong. I told him I was upset about filling out disability forms for the bank, as I felt like a failure. I said I am a failure as a mother and now I am a failure at my job. Something that I was always so proud of, and was such a big part of my life. I wasn't even capable of doing that right. I feel like crawling into a hole. He took me in his arms and tried to comfort me. He tried to reassure me that if I needed to stay off work to help me get better, to do that and not worry what they think. But I am scared.*

Catherine's identity was very much tied with her role at work. And when she quit the job, she felt lost.

> *Friday January 28*
> *How I helped my clients was important to me and how they regarded me as I filled that role was just as important. It is like when they took my position in the branch*

away from me, they tore away a big part of who I was. I feel kind of useless.

As Catherine practised spending more and more time in the Green Zone, she became aware of the incidents and circumstances that pushed her into the Red Zone. So she learned to handle them with caution. One of them was the correspondence from work.

Wednesday February 2
I received another big envelope from work. Maybe it's nothing much but I am taking Dr. Sohail's advice and I am not opening it until I see him Friday.

After making progress in individual and marital therapy, I invited Catherine for group therapy. I was pleasantly surprised that she felt connected with the group members right away and started benefiting from the group experience.

Thursday February 10
I went to my first group therapy session this morning. I didn't really know what to expect because I have never been involved with anything like this before. The small number of people present for my first time made me a little more comfortable. I don't feel quite so alone now. Knowing that there are other people afflicted with problems in life that they are unable to deal with alone makes me feel not quite so different. By different I mean from all the people at work who go on day after day in their own world but never being able to see all the hurting going on inside me. I am relieved that I do not have

to go there every day and try to pretend that life is great, because right now it does not seem that way to me. I am glad Dr. Sohail asked me to come to the group therapy. I am hopeful it will help me.

The more Catherine practised living in the Green Zone, the more she could analyze her own behaviour. It was amazing to see her develop insights and take responsibility for her interactions.

Sunday February 13
After Brent and Colleen had a fight about disciplining their son Evan, I sat in my chair and surveyed the situation. The first thing that came to my mind was that he was using the same parenting methods that I had used with my children. I learned those skills from my parents. I immediately thought: this is an ongoing cycle, but when will it end?

Alongside learning to live in the Green Zone in her day-to-day life, Catherine also started dealing with her parents' death. As she grieved, she felt better and could accept the loss more gracefully. She could gradually let the past go and live in the present.

Thursday February 17
In group therapy the discussion made my mom's death come flooding back to me like it was yesterday. God I miss you, Mom. Why can't I stop missing her? Why can't I let her go? It feels like there is this big hole in my life and there is no way on earth I can fill it. I had to concentrate very hard not to cry in front of everyone.

But now I am alone and I can. My heart keeps breaking over and over and I can't seem to see how to stop it. Sometimes I feel the only time my heart will stop hurting is when I am dead, then I won't be feeling anything. If I told Robert this I think he would probably say, "You just have to get over it, I lost my dad, too." I know that is a sensible and normal way of looking at it, so why can't I do that?

It was encouraging to see Catherine not only connect with other group members but also resolve her issues by identifying through listening to their stories and struggles.

Thursday February 24
I took part in my third group therapy session this morning. When the lady spoke of her granddaughter running away from home all I could think of was the hurt her parents were enduring, and in a moment the tears were running down my cheeks. Though the situation is not exactly the same, the pain hit very close to home and I felt like a failure all over again

Throughout therapy, Catherine's relationship with Monique remained a constant source of support and encouragement. I felt as though Monique and Robert were assisting me in my work.

Wednesday March 1
Monique, Donna and I met at 5 o'clock today at Swiss Chalet. I asked them to come over to our house after we ate. We had a really nice evening. Having all worked together for over ten years, we have shared and seen a

lot. I find the time we spend together very special to me. There is a lot of trust between us and to me, being able to trust a friend is something beyond measure.

I was so impressed by Catherine's descriptions of Monique that I invited her for a session. She seemed more of a family member than many others with whom Catherine did not feel comfortable.

Friday March 3
I was very happy that Monique came with me to meet Dr. Sohail this morning. I think at first she was a little nervous but became fairly comfortable after about ten minutes. She was very honest, as I knew she would be. She has been a good friend. Someone I feel I can really trust, and for me that doesn't come easily. I am normally very suspicious of people and seldom leave myself open to anyone. I guess I feel that if I don't reveal myself, no one can hurt me. I appreciate her coming with me.

In the session, I acknowledged Monique's positive influence on Catherine's progress and thanked her for her support.

Catherine was very nervous that her employer would not approve her disability claim and thus she might find herself in a financial crisis. Although Robert was very supportive, Catherine wanted to be financially self-sufficient and independent. I supported her whole-heartedly and filled out her disability forms. I knew she could not return to that toxic work environment.

Wednesday March 8
Thank God they have approved my long-term disability leave. I don't quite know what I would have done had the result been negative. I am just very relieved that it's been approved. I don't even want to think about having to return to that horrible environment.

As Catherine attended group therapy regularly, she started developing more insights into her family dynamics and her interpersonal relationships. It was a big step for her to become aware of her judgmental attitude and personality and how that pushed her dear ones away.

Thursday March 9
Group was enlightening today. The truth always hurts. The truth is that I am to blame for probably ninety percent of our family problems. Because of my "holier than thou" attitude, I have been successful in driving a lot of people out of my life. My one sister that I no longer talk to hung that description on me a couple of years ago when she had done something to me I found unforgivable. What a group member said sure hit home, when he asked what took place between Laura and me for a 16-year-old to leave home. My poor parenting skills pushed her into becoming something just the opposite of what she was. It's no wonder I can't forgive her for some of the choices she has made ... I can't forgive myself for the ones I made.

Tuesday March 14
Monique and I had lunch today. I told her about my thoughts and feelings after group on Thursday. She told

me to give myself a pat on the back because to look inside myself and realize all those things took a lot of courage. Why don't I feel courageous? I feel like a coward. All I feel for myself is disgust. But I am thankful I have such a true friend, the one who is still standing by me, listening, encouraging, but never judging me.

Catherine gradually started to appreciate that accepting and nurturing others was far healthier than judging and criticizing.

Thursday March 16
I shared feelings today with the group that I did not think I would share with anyone. They listened and shared thoughts, but like Monique, they did not judge me.

As Catherine became aware of her attitude, she was able to restrain herself from falling into the Red Zone. In the beginning, it was hard for her to bite her tongue, but as she saw the benefits, it became easier. It was hard work for her but it was worth it.

Monday March 20
Laura called and told me that they had bought a car. I managed to keep my sarcasm to myself. To change the subject, I then asked her about the girls. I didn't want to stay on the issue of the car. I felt I should quit while the going was still good. I bet I even surprised Laura. She was probably braced for some criticism — but none came. WOW!

When Catherine's relationship with Laura improved, there was less resentment and more affection grew within the relationship. When Laura had interaction with Catherine and left not feeling judged, she started to trust her mother and feel closer to her. The relationship gradually moved from the Red to the Green Zone. Finally there was a loving breakthrough.

> *Sunday March 26*
> *I told Laura I loved her and I shared my regrets about my past. She admitted that it wasn't all my fault, that she had treated us badly as well. I said that we couldn't fix the past but with time and honesty on both sides maybe we could learn to understand and come to grips with it. I told her I wanted to get back the relationship we all once had ... without pretending and always walking around on eggshells all the time. She said she wanted that too. I did not want to go on too long because I wanted the whole conversation to remain positive — for both of us, so I said, "I hope we can talk again just you and I," and with that said I had to go. Before hanging up she paused and said, "I love you, Mom." This time the words sounded like they came right from her heart. When I hung up the phone, I sat there, and could hardly believe what had taken place.*

After resolving the issues with her family, we focused on her work. I realized she could not go back to the bank, so I asked her to do some soul-searching. I wanted her to think about what she enjoyed most in life and what she could foresee doing in the near future that would give her some satisfaction in her day-to-day existence and also make her life more meaningful. As she proceeded in her soul-searching, she got in touch with her inner, deeper self, which was revealed to her in the form of a dream.

> *Friday May 5*
> *Last night I had the strangest dream. Robert and I were down East where his mom lives and we were watching the neighbours drive their herd of cattle from the barn out onto the roadway and into the pasture where they would graze for the day. As we are watching this farmer and his wife move the herd, Robert says, "Well, why don't you ask them if they could use some help doing chores?"*
>
> *I said, "They are going to think I am nuts or something." But I thought what the heck, so I approached the couple and asked them if I could come and work with them on the farm. They both looked at me; the man smiled and his wife tried to speak. I say tried, because she was talking, but though sound was coming out, I could not understand what she was saying. It was like she was talking with marbles in her mouth. Then her husband asked me to come inside where his wife handed me this card (like a greeting card). I was under the impression that if I could read the card I could come and help them on their farm. But the card was a maze of symbols ... no words. I didn't know how to begin to unscramble it. I kept looking at the woman who was still talking, or maybe mumbling is a better word because I wasn't able to understand one word, and then looked down at this card. I seemed to bounce back and forth between the two until I woke up.*

From her dream it was obvious to me that she would enjoy working with animals. She loved animals as she believed they did not judge others. I asked her to volunteer on a farm or with the Humane Society. Catherine wanted to do that but because of her lack of self-confidence, she was reluctant to approach anyone. She was nervous that she would be rejected. Finally she saw an ad in the newspaper and with some encouragement from myself and her friend Monique, took another bold step towards the Green Zone.

Tuesday August 22
I met with Monique for coffee at noon. As we were chatting, Monique, all of a sudden, told me about an ad she cut out of the newspaper on the weekend about someone wanting to hire a person to milk cows. Just then I pulled the ad out of my purse. She was so excited, saying, "That's it. That's it, the same ad!" She immediately asked me if I'd call the people. I said, "Oh God, what will they think?" She said, "They will think you are somebody looking to do the job." I then began going to my negative hiding place and started giving all the reasons why I shouldn't call, but for every one I had against it, she came up with two why I should. She said I had to get rid of my thoughts of "I can't" and make myself believe I "can." Finally with her encouragement, I called and I was accepted for the job.

As Catherine was progressing towards her Green Zone, she was inspired to share her excitement with others. She was transforming from an angry woman to a happy woman right in front of our eyes. It was so wonderful, almost miraculous.

Thursday October 11
The last couple of weeks seemed to have gone by smoothly and quietly, living in the Green Zone. I had everyone over for Thanksgiving dinner on Sunday. We included Robert's brother and his wife and Pam's mom, Mrs. Brady. She was so happy to see us and that we were all together again. She hasn't seen Laura for years but was aware of our troubles. When they brought Mrs. Brady into the house (she was in a wheelchair) and she saw Laura, the two of them hugged so hard I thought they would never let go. Mrs. Brady was crying because she was so happy to see Laura with us. Laura was crying. Pam was crying. I was crying. I think everyone was crying. But they were all happy tears. We had a really good day and shared some happy moments. I was very glad I had included Pam's mom. She doesn't get out much at all and I think she enjoyed the afternoon with all of us.

When we went to bed I lay there a few minutes and said to Robert, "You know I was so happy today. This is how it should be."

He replied, "I felt the same way."

I lay there a bit and said, "I owe so much to Dr. Sohail. Without his help and commitment all this wouldn't be happening. I want him to know I can't believe how much we have accomplished in fourteen months and just how far we have come. Such a long, long way from where we were."

Catherine was very happy working on the farm milking cows and enjoying her family life with her husband, children and grandchildren. She had learned the art of living in her Green Zone. I was so proud of her progress and she was so grateful for the help she received from our clinic.

There were many times I thought of Catherine's dream in which she saw some signs and symbols that she could not decipher. Her dream reminded me of a letter, a story really, that my Israeli friend Lois had shared with me. Before she became an art therapist, she had seen a therapist in America and at the end of therapy had sent him a letter as a last gift. I think that letter, which is copied below, is an excellent expression of the creative and meaningful exchange that takes place between the therapist and the patient in a caring therapeutic relationship.

Dear Friend

There was a small and old book. It was in a corner on a shelf in the library. Most of its pages were glued together and a few of them were torn. The cover was stained and one couldn't read the writer's name. No one knew its content. Sometimes people would glance at it, some people would open it and then put it back, some would get curious about the writer's name but after useless efforts would give up.

One day you stepped into the library, you looked at the book, you turned it over a few times, trying to understand its origin, and to decipher the writer's name. You decided to discover its content. You took all the tools you had. You used all the tools you needed: a lot of water, pins, needles, threads, brushes. You related to every page as if it were a masterpiece, you applied the glue, you let it dry, you added the missing words and only when the page was complete did you go to the next. Once all pages were complete, you put them in the original order, and you sewed one to the other. At the same time you were absorbed in reading the story, paying attention to every simple word because every word was important to you. You were attracted by the big facts and by the small nuances as well. You learned the story and it had a big value to you. You understood its true value. Now the book is complete, the story clear, with a beginning and an end. Now the book is ready to be read by other people, too.

Lois

Part Five

PEOPLE WHO CHOOSE TO LIVE IN THEIR GREEN ZONE

PEOPLE WHO LIVE IN THEIR GREEN ZONE

While I was involved in helping Catherine who lived in the Red Zone for many years prior to receiving therapy then choosing to live in her Green Zone, I was quite impressed by her friend Monique who was a great support for her. She played a significant role in Catherine's rehabilitation. Catherine used to say, "I don't know what I would have done without her." I was so fascinated by Monique's role in Catherine's life and philosophy that I asked to meet her. I found her take on life so interesting that I asked her to write her impressions of Catherine's journey and also share a few glimpses of her own life and philosophy.

Monique's Story

As a little girl we used to play a game called "Red, Yellow, Green Light." When the leader shouted "Red" everyone would stop and stand still. When "Yellow" was yelled you had to walk and when "Green" was called you had to run to try to reach "home" first.

When my friend Catherine was courageous enough to see Dr. Sohail and seek help, it was a time when the essence of her life was very angry and distressed. The day she chose to share with me the simple but so profound concept of "Green, Yellow, and Red Zones" the words reminded me of the game I used to play as a child. Before Catherine went for therapy she was living in the Red Zone. She was choking herself and suffocating the ones close to her. It was really sad to see her suffer so. After she was introduced to the concept of the Zones, she became aware of her behaviour and started to stop and think what Zone she was in. She gradually learned how to recover from functioning in the Red Zone and to restrain herself from falling into the Yellow Zone.

After working hard with this concept, my friend has made a number of changes in her life and is becoming a far happier person. Each day that she restrains herself from the Yellow and Red Zones, she is becoming a stronger person. Now that I look in her eyes, she exudes life that springs from inside her. Now her family, rather than avoiding her, enjoy her company and look forward to their visits. What a remarkable change in her life in just one year!

I would like to thank Dr. Sohail for his guidance with this concept. I can't help wondering how different our society would be if everyone had the opportunity to be exposed to a concept like this one. How might our world be different? I am also thankful to Dr. Sohail to have given me the privilege to be part of this book. This creative project empowers my life in ways I would have never suspected. Dr. Sohail asked me to share my life story so here it is.

I was born in a caring French-Canadian Catholic

family of ten children. What other people thought and said really mattered to us. It was a different world and a different time. Looking back, I just cannot believe that it was just a generation ago.

I grew up in an environment that was very strict, very rigid and without a doubt in mind where men wear the pants. There was no "would", no "could," but a lot of "should." I never felt comfortable saying or doing things I liked. I was aware of all of this at an early age and it shaped my life. I lived a lot of those years in my own private world, in my Yellow Zone, feeling very sad.

I am not sure how this works for other people but for me I did not learn from what I was taught, I learned from what I was not taught. Probably not the best way, or the easiest way to learn, but the only way I found that worked for myself. To this day, this follows me like a shadow; it is part of me. I don't always know what I want but I know what I don't want. I don't always know what to say but I know what not to say. I don't always know where to go, but I know where I don't want to go. To this day I do not tie my shoelaces like anyone else. On my own I found a lifestyle that works for me. My motto to others is, "Find a way that works for you."

When I was of legal age, I left our small town to go to a big city and shut the door on my past. In a big city freedom ranked above all. I had never seen a highway or an overpass. There was a lot of action and I was excited by it all. I was finally starting to breathe on my own. My late teens and early twenties were not filled with the best choices but I was conscious of the process of experimentation and found it interesting. I was curious and open-minded. Those were the years I started to live in my Green Zone.

Going back in time, to the core of this little girl, life was very simple. I remember running from school with a friend all the way home and feeling this was life. I remember jumping fences on a warm summer day and feeling this was life. I remember dreaming of getting and having children and feeling that little voice inside me. It was always there and I was always in tune with it. It was and still is my best friend. I did not need to understand anything about it, it was just part of me.

I met my second best friend in the spring of 1979 and married him in the fall of 1983. His unconditional love made me want to face my blind spots and change into a better person. All thanks go to him for helping me work through the realities and hardships of life. We, as individuals and as a family live most often in the Green Zone.

In life, nothing stays the same. It is a permanent state of adaptation and every day you can make a decision to change your life. I think a lot of us have, and will continue to have, thoughts from childhood that have hurt or that will hurt as an adult. If you want to change with life, you have the choice to change those thoughts and feelings. They belong to the past. I came across a quote that I found helpful in my journey and I have taped it on our bedroom closet door. "Relinquish your need for external approval, you alone are the judge of your worth and your goal is to discover infinite worth in yourself no matter what anyone else thinks. There is great freedom in that realization."

So I began the journey to find what kind of me that I wanted to live with. What kind of wife, mom and friend

I wanted to be. I knew I was surrounded with people who loved me and I loved them. I wanted to live in life's harmony.

My beliefs as an individual are just my beliefs. As an adult I don't have to justify to anyone my choices. I have to live with them. There is great freedom in this realization. You and you alone are responsible for yourself.

My relationship with my partner and family is very open and very simple. We treat each other the way we like to be treated. My emotions were always and always will be a part of me. I have to trust them.

I am an idealistic person and I believe in human nature. In my social life I am very selective whom I let in. More and more I want to surround myself with meaningful relationships. To maintain living in the Green Zone, is what works for me.

One of the blessings of life is that there are so many people around us who are traveling on the path of love and are available to give us strength and to support us in our journey of life through hills and valleys. I am grateful to all those people in my life.

We are all different as human beings. We make mistakes, question ourselves to find meaning in our lives. I believe there is no one way. I believe there is only your way, whatever works for you.

Monique

Monique, in her story, captured the essence of people who live in the Green Zone. Her story is different than the others because she discovered her Green Zone on her own, without therapy, without professional help. For her, her own experiences were her teacher and life itself was the university. In her story, there were significant guiding concepts that resonated with my own philosophy of life and therapy.

A Little Voice . . . My Best Friend

Monique shared her inner thoughts during her story.

> *"The one thing I cherish most from my childhood is that special feeling, that little voice inside me. It was always there and I was always in tune with it. It was and still is my best friend. I did not need to understand anything about it, it was just part of me."*

People who live in the Green Zone are in touch with their inner voice. That voice is their friend, their confidant, and their guide. It is the voice of their Natural Self and keeps them in touch with their true nature. Unfortunately, people who live in the Yellow or Red Zone gradually lose touch with their inner voice and Natural Self. They are more guided by their Conditioned Self, a part of their personality that is more concerned about other people's expectations of them. Such a Conditioned Self is developed when children are told at every step what they "should do," "must do," and "have to do." The more religious, traditional and conservative the family, the more opportunities for this dictatorial process to happen. Since Monique grew up in a strict, patriarchal Catholic family she fully experienced that environment. She wrote,

> *"What other people thought and said really mattered ... I grew up in an environment that was very strict, very rigid ... there was no* would, *no* could *and a lot of* should. *I never felt comfortable saying or doing things I liked."*

In spite of Monique's family being traditional it was still caring, so Monique never lost her inner voice. After living in the Yellow Zone with her family as a child, when she got an opportunity as a young adult to fully discover herself, she started living in the freedom of her Green Zone.

Children who grow up in families where there is a lot of abuse or neglect are vulnerable to losing touch with their inner voice and to doubting their own thoughts, feelings and choices in life. Those are the people who rediscover their inner voice in therapy. As they start trusting their inner voice they become their own best friends and take their lives into the happiness found in the Green Zone.

Second Best Friend

Monique described her husband as her second best friend, her inner voice being the first. How remarkable to put herself first but in a most non-selfish way. I was intrigued by her perspective. She reminded me of many women I have worked with who never trusted their inner voice, who were never their own best friends and when they found a lover or a spouse they considered them their first best friend. Unfortunately if they lost them by death or divorce, they fell apart and became extremely depressed.

Monique's description of her husband as her second best friend also highlighted that she was emotionally strong and independent. She also described the relationship quite succinctly,

> *"His unconditional love made me want to face my blind spots and change into a better person. All thanks go to him for helping me to work through the realities and hardships of life."*

People living in the Green Zone have discovered such friends, male or female, who accept them unconditionally and with whom they can grow in life. Sometimes such a friend becomes a spouse, but even in those intimate relationships, friendship is the cake and the romance and sex is the icing. That is why even if they have to separate in life they can still maintain their friendship and treat each other with respect. Such a friendship keeps them from becoming angry, resentful and bitter.

Mutual Respect in the Family

Monique not only lives in the Green Zone with herself and her husband, she has also discovered a Green Zone family environment.

> *"My relationship with my partner and family is very open and very simple. We treat each other the way we like to be treated. We, as individuals and as a family, live mostly in the Green Zone."*

Families who live in the Green Zone have a mixture of nurturing and setting limits. Everybody feels loved but are also able to negotiate their needs. In Monique's description, the expression "mostly" is significant. When people live together, it is not realistic to expect that they would always be in their Green Zone. They visit Yellow and Red Zones but do not remain. Their crises provide them with an opportunity to come close and grow together. Even when family members are upset and angry, they are still respectful towards each other.

Leaving The Past Behind

People who live in their Green Zone have learned to overcome past hurts and painful experiences. They can transcend their yesterdays to live in their todays. They can live in the present and find a purpose in their day-to-day life. Monique's comment is significant,

> *"I think a lot of us have and will have thoughts from childhood that have hurt or that will hurt as an adult. If you want to change with life, you have the choice to change those thoughts and feelings. They belong to the past."*

Those who choose to live in their Green Zone find a purpose in their day-to-day existence in which they discover a much more meaningful lifestyle.

MY LIFE AND DREAM

Mike, the life partner of one of my patients, was a very nurturing and supportive man. However, after meeting him I realized that he had lived in the Red Zone most of his life but after a startling dream he was transformed. He was very well respected in the community and a source of inspiration for many. I requested him to share his story with me.

Dr. Sohail

From a very young age I felt that no one loved me and my esteem was at a low point. My father was abusive and my mother worked at a time when most moms were at home. I never saw my parents hug or show any affection towards each other, let alone offer any to me.

I believe my life of anger and violence started when at the age of seven, four or five older boys jumped me and beat me quite bad. My head was swollen and I had double vision for months. Following the attack I also had to wear an eye patch for months, which led to even more mocking from my peers, causing me to resort to violence to get a false sense of respect. It was only later in life that I realized the difference between fear and respect.

As I grew older I tried several ways to channel my anger such as boxing and joining the army. This was the start of my addiction to alcohol and led to drugs as well. I was thrown out of the army with dishonor, after I struck a superior officer.

I spent the next ten years spiraling lower and lower in the Red Zone until the paranoia was so bad I would sit on the floor in the corner of my room with a gun on my lap doing whatever drugs I could score. My anger and abuse cost me two marriages and the opportunity to watch my two sons grow up. My abusing drugs also led me to jail and institutions.

The start of my new birth, my living in the Green Zone, after living in the Red Zone most of my life was because of the dream I had. It was so real to me that even today I am not even sure it was a dream. I saw that I woke up in a coffin and the room was very bright and quiet. I, for some reason, sat up to find an empty room with a podium at the front just behind my coffin. Somehow I got up and walked to the podium to deliver my own eulogy only to find out that I could not think of one good thing to say. It was at that time I started to cry and decided I had to do something. I realized that the worst thing in life is not only to be alone but to die alone and not even be missed.

Since that time I joined Narcotics Anonymous and carried the message to jails and treatment centers. For many years I dedicated myself to helping others with their addictions. I am not sure how many others I have helped; I only know that doing this gave me a feeling of self-worth. It was a few years later that I met my soul-mate and found what I believe to be true love and respect.

Sincerely,
Mike

DISCOVERING ONE'S GREEN ZONE

An interview with Dr. Sohail

It is a rare occasion indeed when an editor becomes so emboldened in his wrap-up of work with a special client, that he is unknowingly reserving space in the author's book.

So fascinated had I become with Dr. Sohail's outlook on life, while working on two prior publications he'd written, that I found myself thinking guardedly before asking the following question. "Sohail," I enquired, using the name he prefers, "interviewing and analyzing is the raison d'être of your profession and, although I cannot participate in your sessions as an observer, I am intrigued enough in the topic to ask that the roles be reversed with you becoming the interviewee."

Sohail smiled and I could see his eyes sparkle at the challenge. "Let me probe into the thinking that brought about the Green, Yellow, Red Zones manuscript using questions I'll devise as if I were a journalist engaging you in a formal interview."

Even though we'd spent months on rewriting, editing and proofreading this new book, he knew I was ever curious to get him to further explain his underlying views that created the oeuvre of the philosophy that brought the Green, Yellow, Red Zones into such a prominent place in his practice.

We put off such a session until I had collected questions without his interjection so that the formal interview would allow me to delve into the topic, yet seek out answers that would be spontaneous.

Later that week my query turned into a most intriguing session, that, surprising to me and at the insistence of Dr. Sohail, found a place in this publication.

With his wonderful ability to recall, Sohail put the session on paper and required, over my ever-weakening protestations, that it be used so others would enjoy the Green, Yellow, Red Zone lessons of the dialogue.

We hope you do.

Bill Belfontaine

⌛

Bill: I have read the fascinating stories of those men and women who discovered a happy and healthy lifestyle using the concept of Green, Yellow and Red Zones. Can you share with me how this philosophic journey begins?

Sohail: Like any profound journey it starts with baby steps. We all must learn to crawl before we can walk and we have to learn to walk before we can run. I share with my friends and clients that life is not a one hundred-meter sprint, they are on a marathon run and we have to adopt the philosophy of a marathon runner to be happy and successful in life. To be successful, marathoners learn patience and pacing to assure they maintain their endurance and the pace that will take them to the finish line. One cannot afford to run too fast, as slow and steady and measured steps are needed to win the race. That is why I use turtles in my clinical practice as symbols of the therapeutic journey as turtles walk slowly and live long. Over the centuries they have acquired a special place in the world's mythology and folklore.

I caution people to keep their journey simple and to start it with a Green Hour each day. Within that hour I encourage them to discover their Natural Self which is essential if one wants to live in the Green Zone. I share with them that our personalities have different parts. We all have a Conditioned Self which is the result of the conditioning done by our families and schools in our childhood. A Conditioned Self is guided by *should*, *must*, and *have to*. On the other hand our Natural Self is guided by *like to*, *want to*, and *love to*.

So I encourage them to do things in that Green Zone Hour that they would *like* to do, *want* to do and *love* to do rather than what they *should* do, *must* do or *have to* do. In the beginning they feel bad or guilty as old thinking dies slowly, but as they get used to it they start enjoying it without a feeling of guilt. It then becomes easier for them to extend a Green Zone Hour to a Green Zone Afternoon, then onward into a Green Zone Day and a Green Zone Weekend. Last week one of my patients was thrilled to share with me that for the first time in a long while she had a Green Zone Week. It was like a miracle of change and enlightenment to her.

B: *How do people living in the Green Zone cope with the people and environments of those who live in the Red Zone? Surely having to live, socialize, sympathize or work with Red Zone people — can I use the term sufferers? — requires a steadfast determination not to be dragged into their mood?*

S: The first step is to recognize those people and environments and after recognizing them to encourage the donning of an "Emotional Raincoat" before interacting with those who are trying to deal with life in the Red Zone. Such mental protection is necessary to shield oneself from other people's Red Zone activities. It takes a firm resolve to be the ruler of your interaction with them. Those people who have developed an Emotional Raincoat can also enter Red Zone Environments and be minimally affected by them. Wearing an Emotional Raincoat is no different than those police officers who wear a bullet proof vest before they go out on the street or into a dangerous situation. It makes them feel secure. It is also like many people who put a sun block on before they sun bathe to protect them from becoming harmed by the heat and rays of the sun.

B: *Would you please expand on your example of how one wears an Emotional Raincoat.*

S: Do you mind if I make this answer personal? There are many times when I like to visit my friends in the west end of Toronto. Travelling in rush hour means there is a lot more traffic with its slower pace and often quick stops and slow starts. I am aware that if I got stuck in traffic I might become frustrated and move from my usual Green Zone outlook into a Yellow or Red Zone. Here is where my favourite music tapes are used to help me get through my crosstown journey. Those tapes act like an Emotional Raincoat for me, taking the stress out of the delay caused by the time that I think is lost.

On a less personal note, one of my patients loves her brother but does not get along with her sister-in-law. She likes to avoid her but if she cannot do that physically, she distances herself emotionally to protect herself from being shaken out of her Green Zone. Once she told me, "When she comes into the room, I mentally leave." Such an action, dramatic as it may seem, acts like an Emotional Raincoat. By recognizing such people and situations, and finding ways to satisfactorily cope with them in advance, gives people more control in their daily lives and they start taking greater responsibility for their well-being and mental health.

B: *How do you help people to change their outlook so they can enjoy the harmony of living in Green Zone relationships?*

S: First I urge people to start at the beginning, which is to create a list of all the significant relationships in their life and then to carefully and thoughtfully review each one to determine who lives in a Green, Yellow or Red Zone. Green Zone relationships are sincere and based on genuine friendships in which both parties affectionately bring out the best in each other. Friends are, most often, a good support network, but they too have shortcomings which must be recognized.

Once people observe and document the Yellow and Red relationships in which they feel anxious, frustrated, angry and resentful, I encourage them to write a letter to those people inviting them to discuss the possibility of having a Green Zone relationship. The future health of any significant relationship depends upon whether both parties are able to work at finding and resolving the conflicts. If people can agree to improve their relationship on their own or with the help of a mediator or a therapist, then the future becomes very positive for them. Therapy helps people realize that relationships are more important than maintaining negative issues at hand. Good friends must be able to agree to disagree and respect each other's points of view and philosophies without loss of the connection that makes them good friends. Such understanding can deepen their relationships in future.

But, if the other party is very self-righteous and wants to impose values and lifestyles, then I encourage people to dissolve the relationship and say goodbye to Yellow and Red Zone relationships. Some people feel relieved after such a decision is taken while others are quite saddened by it. It is interesting to see how those people who feel sad, after grieving the relationship, are ready to initiate and maintain a new Green Zone relationship with a new friend, lover or even a spouse. There are some occasions in which it is not realistic to dissolve the relationship. In such cases I ask them to accept the situation and wear an Emotional Raincoat as a shield against losing their position in the Green Zone. The example of the woman I quoted earlier who loved her brother but did not get along with her sister-in-law highlighted such a situation.

B: *How do you encourage people to deal with their Yellow and Red Zone Families?*

S: They must recognize the difference between Loving and Business relationships. In my mind, relationships between friends, lovers, spouses and family members are Loving relationships. Such connections should be kept sincere, caring and affectionate. In such relationships people share whatever they can with their loved ones without worrying about the returns. On the other hand, their Business relationships are based on fairness and justice and there are mutual material expectations and when those expectations are not met there is a conflict and finally disappointment and even separation in the relationship. Over the years I have seen many Green Zone families regress to Yellow and Red Zone families when Loving relationships become transformed into Business relationships.

One of my patients is the mother of a teenager. She shared with me that her son lives in the basement of her house and she had asked him to pay rent of $200 a month.

"Why?" I asked.

"Because I want him to become responsible. If I rented the basement I would have been able to ask $400 a month but I am only asking him for $200." Then she paused for a second, as if feeling guilty, and said, "I am not going to use his money for myself. I plan to save it and return it to him to pay his tuition fees when he enters university."

"The day you accept his rent, you would no longer be a nurturing, caring and loving mother, you will become a landlady and he will turn into a tenant and sooner or later his respect and love for you will be undermined."

My patient, like many other parents, who mean well but are naïve, did not see my point. For the first three months everything was fine and my patient was happy. The fourth month the son paid only $100. When she asked the reason he said, "I wasn't here for the entire month, I spent two weeks with my girl friend." The fifth month he again paid $100 and said, "I no longer eat at home. So you are saving money on food." Within six months the Loving Relationship regressed to the Red Zone. Not only that, the son moved out and they have not spoken to each other since.

I shared with the mother that if her son had learned to love and respect his mother for her many contributions toward raising him, he would have contributed and helped her without her asking for a fixed rent. Unfortunately, by the time the mother appreciated my advice it was too late. I see too many of these tragedies with couples and families.

B: *Yellow and Red Zone Work environments can be very destructive. How do you help people to cope with the problems they encounter in these negative situations?*

S: I encourage people to ask themselves if the work brings out the best in them and whether they feel comfortable with their colleagues and bosses. Many people need support to fight for their rights and privileges. If there is no hope for change, I encourage them to explore their options and choices.

B: *I assume you've been in such situations, too?*

S: Let me share one with you. I worked in a psychiatric

hospital where, for the first ten years I loved it, as I was working in a Green Zone Environment. But then a number of political changes occurred in the administration. I felt those changes came about because of financial reasons and not as a concern for better patient care. With such changes the staff became more frustrated, angry and resentful of actions taken by the administration and bureaucracy. The environment gradually became toxic. When I realized that I was incompatible with the institution, I decided to leave and requested my colleague, Anne, who I respected as a psychiatric nurse, to work with me to open a psychotherapy clinic. I receive less income but have a greater peace of mind. I love being at the clinic to counsel people needing help. I encourage people to review their priorities at work.

Sometimes we have to sacrificc smaller goals for bigger goals. Sometimes we must sacrifice financial status for a happiness that money could never buy.

Many people have come to us who were sad and depressed when they lost a job but after recovery they either went back to school to be retrained or started a career they would never have imagined if they had not lost their job in the first place. One of my friends, who was a millionaire, encountered numerous problems and ended up bankrupt. But he did not give up or give in. After a decade he worked his way back and is a millionaire again, a successful businessman. When I asked his secret he said, "I believed if I could be a millionaire once, I could do it again." Many times break***downs*** can be transformed into break***throughs*** with the right attitude and support.

B: *Would you expand your views about Yellow and Red Zone Communities? I've been there myself and never acquired or developed the insight to be able to deal with their negative influences completely.*

S: Lucky are those who are born and brought up in Green Zone Communities. Such communities respect secular and humanistic values, meaning that people from all cultures and religions are equally respected. My early and formative years were spent in a very conservative, traditional and religious environment where my non-conventional thinking and non-traditional lifestyle were not respected and appreciated. I was always apprehensive of the repercussions that could affect myself, and especially my family if I broke with tradition.

In the beginning I formed a circle of like-minded friends, I like to call them "my family of the heart," to cope with such an environment; but when the social and political conflicts escalated to the point that I started feeling like a stranger in my own home and homeland, I left the country experiencing the difficulty of leaving family and friends. After coming to Canada, I felt as if I were living in a Green Zone Community, although I didn't call it that back then because of certain hardships. But what a difference it made!

We have to work hard to create the environment where people appreciate each other's differences and maintain the realization that we are all members of the human family. To create Green Zone Communities, we have to break down the walls of prejudice and bridge the moats of misunderstanding to create empathy and compassion for the way other people live. We have to promote Humanistic values that support equality in our homes, schools, social environments and workplaces.

It is important for people to differentiate between rights and privileges. In the 1980s when Nelson Mandela was still in prison, one of my South African friends of Asian descent was asked by another Canadian friend, "How are Asians treated in South Africa?"

He replied, "We do not have the same privileges as Whites."

"They have really brainwashed you," she said, surprised.

"What do you mean?" he looked puzzled.

"You are calling rights your privileges. Going to school, voting and free mobility in your own country are rights, not privileges."

That day I realized how important it is to educate even the educated and raise their social consciousness so that Green Zone Communities become established and flourish world-wide.

B: How can people discover and maintain a Green Zone lifestyle for themselves?"

S: To live a Green Zone lifestyle, one has to discover a purpose, a sense of direction and a special meaning in life. I ask people in numerous ways to think deeply as they ask of themselves:

"What has been your dream all your life?"

"What did you always want to accomplish?"

"What did you always want to do?"

"When you were a teenager, what did you fantasize you would become later in life?"

Many shared their dreams and I can still see the

smiles that started in their eyes and radiated to their faces. I could see I had hit a responsive chord that was part of their natural spiritual demeanor.

But then there were others whose faces remained blank, eyes empty, unable to find the words in their closed hearts and minds to answer such questions. I always thought it was tragic they have never had a dream, or a star to follow, or if they had, they lost it while working to survive. I do not mean a dream of chauffer-driven Rolls Royce cars, but simple dreams that can add so much to their lives. But they were so overwhelmed by their day-to-day struggle, which had become suffering rather than a challenge, that they didn't have the emotional strength to reach out their hand to touch the fabric of opportunity that would have created, or recreated, their dreams. With such people I work hard to offer them hope, to help them accept the hope that is needed if they are to discover a new dream, a new meaning in life.

Over the years I found there are three paths that lead to the Green Zone lifestyle. They join each other at different points in the journey that I ask my patients to undertake. They are: Creativity, Spirituality, and Serving Humanity.

To begin the journey to Creativity, the first step is to discover a special interest in life. All children enjoy playing but too few adults allow themselves to smile, laugh, and be playful and to use humor to feel a solid part of life. This special interest can be related to any aspect of life. Such interests give birth to worthwhile hobbies. Some begin with a visit to the library, some pursue a special sport, some join friends in special projects, others undertake a special reading program to gain the strength to move forward. As time passes, those special interests and hobbies will grow to become more meaningful and gradually transform into a passion. Developing that passion, that interest, is the first step to pursuing a dream and to exposing that special gift to others and ourselves that we all have waiting inside.

People with passion are energized and motivated. They move beyond the mundane activities and relationships we all encounter. It gives them a focus, a sense of direction, a direction that is guided by their hearts rather than traditions; that is created by their Natural Self rather than their Conditioned Self with its restrictions and confining rules. Such freedom leads to happiness, and tranquility becomes available to enjoy a newly-found peace of mind.

Creativity can be expressed in everyday life, in acts of cooking, baking, knitting, sewing, interior decoration, working in a garden, creating games with children and the thousands of other activities open to us all. For some, their creativity is expressed in creative arts, whether they be poems or stories, songs or paintings to create and enjoy. Even those people who suffer from a lot of pain in their hearts and carry souls burdened with sorrow, I encourage them to read the biographies of artists like Vincent Van Gogh and Freida Kahlo, and writers like Virginia Woolf, who chose to transform their pain into paintings and their sufferings into lines of literature. They gradually realize that the hardships of these famous artists became the raw material for their masterpieces. We named our place of healing, "Creative Psychotherapy Clinic" to inspire our patients to pursue their creative potential so that they can become lotuses that transcend the bogs of their Red Zone Environments.

My own creative efforts in the Green Zone have helped me grow as a writer as well as enjoying my days helping people as a psychotherapist.

The second pathway to a Green Zone lifestyle is that of Spirituality. I encourage people to engage their minds in soul-searching. That helps them to leave the highway of tradition and follow the trail of their hearts into new meaning. Institutions can be extremely suffocating and restricting. I urge everyone to read mystic poetry and biographies of mystics so that they can see how mystics transcend the religious, social and cultural institutions so they can find the freedom that comes from discovering their own truths.

B: *In your book* From Isalm to Secular Humanism, A Philosophical Journey, *you have focused on the lives of mystics and their humanistic philosophy and quoted Walt Whitman's poetry. Why is this so important to understand?*

S: Many mystics, alongside creating, what I call, wisdom literature, also found ways to serve humanity. Walt Whitman was one such personality. He had discovered the bridge where passion embraces compassion and creativity joins hands with the desire to serve humanity, and that is the third pathway to a Green Zone lifestyle.

B: *So mysticism, often seen in North America as an Eastern practice, is really part of everyone if we choose to use it. Is there a special section in the book you would like to share to emphasize this point?*

S: Precisely. Let me read these few paragraphs to you: "Mystics have always been compassionate toward common people. Their doors and hearts are always open to people from all walks of life. They try to help the needy and poor, and offer support to the sick and disabled. It is not uncommon to see mystics working as nurses, doctors and voluntary workers in clinics and hospitals, offering their services whenever communities need them.

Mother Teresa was an excellent example of a mystic who selflessly served the poor and the sick for half a century.

Walt Whitman a mystic poet offered his services to the Soldier's Hospital in Washington during the American Civil War in the 1800s. A friend wrote about one of his visits to the hospital. "Never shall I forget that visit ... to one he gave a few words of cheer, for another he wrote a letter home, to others he gave an orange, a few comfits [sugar confection], a cigar, a pipe and tobacco, a sheet of paper or a postage stamp, all of which, and many other things, were in his capacious haversack ... he did the things for them which no nurse or doctor could do, and he seemed to leave a benediction at every cot as he passed along. He performed miracles, the doctors said, miracles of healing.

Many of the soldiers remembered him years later as 'The man with the face of a Saviour.' Walt Whitman wrote a beautiful poem describing his feeling at the sight of a slain enemy.

> *"For my enemy is dead, a man divine as myself is dead*
> *I look where he lies white-faced and stiff in the coffin ... I draw near*
> *Bend down and touch lightly with my lips the white face in the coffin."*

B: *But there are people who serve others who often reach the point of being burnt out.*

S: There are two types of service that people offer their loved ones and humanity. One is offered out of a sense of duty and obligation. They feel they *have to* or *should* or *must* serve others. Many such examples are found in parents who look after children and sacrifice their lives at home, or workers who dedicate their lives to their workplace out of a strong sense of obligation. Such a sense of duty and moral obligation backfires in many cases. After some time, when people misuse and abuse themselves, they start feeling tired, irritable and exhausted, and then anger arises and they become resentful and even bitter. Some reach the point of feeling burnt out very quickly, or it may take several years depending on their spiritual stamina. They may never recover to re-enter what was once a healthy, chosen lifestyle for them.

The second type of service is cheerfully carried out because it is rendered by people who are motivated by the expressions *like to* and *want to* and *love to*. Such actions are expressions of love for others.

Over the years my colleague Anne, who loves to do volunteer work, has made me realize its significance. I became aware that the best way to discover one's Green Zone lifestyle is by doing voluntary work and serving humanity. To serve others, we do not need the higher learning that comes with a Ph.D. in Sociology or Philosophy, or a Masters Degree in Psychology or Anthropology. One can participate in their community, offering joy and companionship by reading to a blind man, or taking an elderly woman for her doctor's appointment, or visiting children in an orphanage. By helping others we rise above our own difficulties, and connect with others in a positive and meaningful way. In many people their creative, spiritual and voluntary activities help them build bridges of caring among people, families and communities which is an expression that comes from their firmly-planted roots in their Green Zones.

When we read the biographies of scientists, artists, mystics and social reformers, we find that many had discovered their Green Zone. They continually sacrificed because they believed in their dream, their goal, and their mission. Nelson Mandela, who lived for years in a prison on Robben Island in South Africa, transformed it into a Green Zone, an island of peace and hope surrounded by its ocean of ignorance, poverty, prejudice and suffering. He dealt with his problems gracefully. That is why, in spite of all that he faced, he never became bitter.

People who can transform their Green Zones into Green Islands like Canadian Terry Fox, India's Mother Teresa, America's Martin Luther King Jr. and South Africa's Nelson Mandela discover the secret of living peacefully in their hearts and serving humanity the best way they can. I present those people as role-models especially for those who do not have positive and inspiring role-models in their own families and communities.

B: *I am much more enlightened having spent this time with you. Would you please summarize so I can go with a succinct message to dwell upon in future?*

Sohail: I strongly feel that people's creativity, spirituality and their desire to serve humanity give them a special meaning in life. Discovering a Green Zone lifestyle helps us to grow stronger as individuals while we are serving the Community. It helps us make our tomorrows better than our yesterdays.

Such a Humanistic Philosophy makes us healthier and happier human beings and that is the reason that this book is dedicated to all those who choose to free themselves from the past by taking their first step in the direction that will take them into a place of tranquility, their Green Zone.

Bill: *Thank You.*

Part Six

YOUR SELF-ASSESSMENT QUESTIONNAIRE

YOUR SELF-ASSESSMENT QUESTIONNAIRE

Over the years we have developed a questionnaire that is interesting and revealing, yet quite simple to complete that will introduce you to our concept of your Green Yellow Red Zones. It will help you to discover for yourself the strength and weaknesses of your personality and lifestyle. It will also help you to decide whether you need professional assistance to improve your quality of life.

The Green Zone

When people choose to live in the Green Zone they are, amongst many other things, pleasant and cheerful. They easily carry on a rational discussion with those around them and should a difference of opinion arise, they are able to enthusiastically connect with a healthy and constructive inner strength that will encourage the dialogue that helps to resolve or dissolve their conflicts — and most importantly — build bridges across all differences.

The Yellow Zone

When in the Yellow Zone people feel distressed. Anxiety, sadness and anger too often rule their thoughts and actions. Because of their discomfort, they are unable to communicate with others properly and are poorly equipped to deal with stressful situations or interpersonal conflicts. This Zone is a slippery slope that often leads into many problems that await them when they fall into the Red Zone.

The Red Zone

Those who occupy the Red Zone are extremely unhappy, emotionally exhausted, usually maintaining a high state of hidden anger and are continually distressed. They often lose control and become abusive or completely withdrawn from others, sometimes fleeing to escape — even from themselves! They have great difficulty dealing with stressful situations, unable to have a rational discussion to resolve or dissolve their interpersonal conflicts. At times they lack the will to take care of their personal appearance, overlook proper nourishment and avoid being responsible for family members in their charge.

Questionnaire

To help everyone to understand just where they are located within the three Zones, a questionnaire follows that will greatly assist you to better understand the rationale within the pages of this book.

Completing your questionnaire

We suggest you begin by making a work copy of the following questionnaire pages.

Record your answers in pencil on the work pages. Be fair, open and honest with yourself as you make your entries. Don't hurry; think carefully before you record your opinions. When in doubt, be wise by making your temporary comments subject to a later review to assure you make the best contribution possible to this personal assessment.

During later review, when you are rewriting from your worksheet copies to the original, you will want to add or delete information so that your answer is clearer. We encourage you to do so. This is not the time to be impatient. If space is limited on the questionnaire and it would be helpful as you feel you want to write more, please use additional pages, rather than the back of these sheets, for expanded comments because the process of writing is very valuable to you. For instance you may have had Green Zone years but that changed and needs explanation to assure it is understood properly by you when you read it at a later date. Take your time; you may be looking at paper right now, but in actual fact you are looking down the path to a better life. Let this questionnaire be another step along the way. Your first one was reading this book.

Best wishes
K. Sohail

Questionnaire

1) What Zone colours have you lived in most of your life? (If more than one, use a percentage figure to show the comparison.)

	Green	Yellow	Red
Up to 15 years			
16 to 30			
31 to present			

2) In what Zones do you presently spend your time?

	Green	Yellow	Red
Mostly			
Occasionally			
Rarely			

3) What Zones do you presently live in within your family environment?

	Green	Yellow	Red
Mostly			
Occasionally			
Rarely			

4) In your work environment, what Zones do you presently live in?

	Green	Yellow	Red
Mostly			
Occasionally			
Rarely			

5) In your present social environment what Zones do you live in?

	Green	Yellow	Red
Mostly			
Occasionally			
Rarely			

6) If needed, what three things can you do to recover from Yellow and Red Zones?
   a.
   b.
   c.

7) What are the three most important things you can do to restrain yourself from falling into the Yellow and Red Zones?
   a.
   b.
   c.

8a. List all your significant relationships and then decide in what Zone each lives.

	Name	Relationship	Green	Yellow	Red
1					
2					
3					
4					
5					
6					

7 ______________________________
8 ______________________________
9 ______________________________
10 ______________________________
11 ______________________________
12 ______________________________
13 ______________________________
14 ______________________________
15 ______________________________
16 ______________________________
17 ______________________________
18 ______________________________

8b. With which significant relationships can you comfortably discuss the concept of Green Yellow Red Zones in the hope of improving the quality of that relationship? (Please refer to item 8a above and circle the appropriate numbers.)

8c. In which significant relationships can you discuss the issue of finding a Mediator or a Therapist? (Please go back to item 8a above and add a square box to the appropriate numbers.)

8d. Which significant relationships can you dissolve (have little or no communication with in future) because there is no hope or willingness to resolve conflicts in order improve the quality of the relationships? (Please go back to item 8a above and draw an X through the appropriate numbers.)

9. List social, professional, political, religious communities, and cultural organizations you belong to and then decide the Zone you live in with each one.

Name	Green	Yellow	Red
1			
2			
3			
4			
5			
6			
7			
8			
9			
10			
11			
12			
13			
14			
15			

10. What five things can you do to live regularly in the Green Zone?

a. ______________________

b. ______________________

c. ______________________

d. ______________________

e. ______________________

11. Do you need professional help to live in the Green Zone? Explain why.

FINALE

When you live in the Green Zone during most aspects of your life, you are very likely leading a happy, healthy and balanced life. When the Yellow Zone causes pain during most aspects of your life, you need to think seriously how you can improve the quality of your life by discussing it with significant others. When the Red Zone dominates your life, you need to seriously consider seeking professional counselling to bring fulfillment and joy into your life.

Green, Yellow, Red.
What will be the colour
that you let shine upon your life?

DISCOVERING YOUR GREEN DAY

Name	**Day**	**Date**
	GREEN / YELLOW / RED ZONES	
Morning		
Afternoon		
Evening		
Night		

DISCOVERING YOUR GREEN WEEK

DATE	HOURS IN EACH ZONE			
DAYS	**GREEN**	**YELLOW**	**RED**	**COMMENTS**
Monday				
Tuesday				
Wednesday				
Thursday				
Friday				
Saturday				
Sunday				

What people say whose lives were changed by "*The Art of Living in Your Green Zone*."

"Sohail's book is a clear, caring service to humanity. It has been valuable for me because of the simple guidelines and tools he provides for implementing his experience-derived concepts.

Decades of providing good training have proven to me that humans need tools not just concepts when they want to make changes." ~ Warren McCarthy, Founder, Effectivation Inc.

⌛

"As you will learn in this highly readable book, *The Art Of Living In Your Green Zone*, the general principles of leading a happy productive life full of harmonious relationships, are accessible to everyone.

Read this book carefully and use it as a blueprint to build positive moments, hours, days and weeks." ~ Leslie James

⌛

"Overwhelmed by stress? Need help to cope with your life? Dr. Sohail's, *The Art of Living in Your Green Zone* is a great book to raise your level of awareness of your emotional triggers. It also helps you to develop the skills needed to successfully deal with difficult situations, to give you peace of mind.

The personal stories from the people he has assisted have a powerful effect by helping you to identify your specific problems of overreaction, and provide ways to maintain a calm outlook that will remove debilitating stress from your life. Every story of an individual's pain and later success gives genuine hope to those who feel emotionally overburdened and burnt out.

And finally, the practical worksheets at the end of the book allow you to focus on identifying and finding strategies to help solve problems that concern you." ~ Amanda

⌛

"I feel fortunate to have read *The Art of Living In Your Green Zone*. I am a visual person so this deceptively easy but powerful concept allows me to see myself, and others, in a new light—or perhaps I should say colour. I more clearly understand the choices I make to stay in a given zone or move to another. This gives me a sense of control over how the events of any given day will impact on me.

While reading Dr. Sohail's book, I felt Viktor Frankl, the eminent Viennese psychotherapist, was sitting right alongside me. To me he is the epitome of someone who has created and experienced his Green Zone and was determined to stay in it even though it would be impacted by indescribably hideous circumstances. In his book, *Man's Search for Meaning*, Frankl tells us that while he had survived Auschwitz, his mother, father, brother, and pregnant wife were all murdered by the Nazis. He lost everything he valued in life, except one thing: The last of the human freedoms to choose one's attitude in any given set of circumstances. *The Art of Living in Your Green Zone* provides simple, yet dynamic directions to help us create our unflinching resolve and ability to remain, as Frankl did, in our Green Zone." ~ Sandra Manuel, Poetess

⌛

I was very impressed with the introduction of Dr. Sohail's life events that brought him to this place as a top-notch psychotherapist/psychiatrist. Having stated his background and progression of studies and work, there is a strong credibility to his knowledge and application of theories that proves itself throughout the book, by common sense and through the personal testaments.

The concept of Green, Yellow and Red zones enables us to visualize the places where we live, moment to moment, day to day. Everyone, in their teens and twenties, should read this book. Readers will have a far better understanding of themselves and the dynamics of their relationships.

Awareness is key to understanding, and Dr. Sohail's concept enables us to become much more aware. People generally float with the flow within their existence until a crisis causes them to flounder — and they exhaust themselves treading water, going nowhere. Given the emotional and communication skills acquired by recognizing and practicing the concept of the "Zones" at an early age can, would enable anyone to develop good coping skills as they develop into adult life. Fostered in youth, these gifts have the strength to guide us through the rapids of life by swimming with confidence in every kind of emotional water.

This book has been very valuable to me. I will continue to use the awareness raised in me for the rest of my life ... and I will bring the message to others, too. Just knowing the things that are the triggers in your life and how to deal with them in order to stay in the Green Zone is very helpful. Recognizing and reevaluating is key to solving any problem, and this concept explains how to step back and analyze, recognize and restore one's behaviour and outlook — it encourages one to use their ability to change, enhance and be happier with themselves and others. ~ Diana Plitz